During World War II the U.S. Navy produced a re-markable group of swimming warriors often called frogmen.

As volunteers for extra hazardous duty, these men carried out vital pre-invasion assignments in such major offensives as Saipan, Guam, Iwo Jima and Okinawa. They charted the approaches to enemy beaches and destroyed mines and other obstacles that could block the path of American landing craft.

In this book Wyatt Blassingame describes the daring World War II exploits of the Underwater Demolition Teams—the U.S. Navy frogmen.

The U.S. Frogmen
of World War II

John Higgins

The U.S. Frogmen of World War II

Wyatt Blassingame

illustrated with photographs
and maps

Random House
New York

Grateful acknowledgment is made to:

Holt, Rinehart and Winston, Inc. for permission to use on pages
103–04 a quotation from BATTLE REPORT, VICTORY IN THE
PACIFIC. Prepared from Official Sources by Captain Walter Karig,
USNR; Lieutenant Commander Russell L. Harris, USNR and Lieu-
tenant Commander Frank A. Manson, USN. Holt, Rinehart and
Winston, Inc. as publishers.

Appleton-Century-Crofts for permission to use on page 17 a quotation from THE NAKED WARRIORS by Commander Francis
Douglas Fane and Don Moore. The author is also most grateful
to Appleton-Century-Crofts, Inc. for permitting him to use from
this most interesting book about U.S. Navy frogmen certain points
of information not readily available elsewhere.

All photographs in this book are from the U.S. Navy with the exception
of the following: Pix, page 24; Imperial War Museum, page 35; Colonel
John T. O'Neill, pages 52 (bottom), 56; United Press International, pages
42–43, 60, 89 (right), 122, 150; U.S. Army, page 52 (top); U.S. Coast
Guard, pages 2, 48, 108; U.S. Marine Corps, pages 38, 82, 118; Wide
World, pages 19, 30, 36, 71.

Cover photograph courtesy of the U.S. Navy

Library of Congress Catalog Card Number: 64-11175

Manufactured in the United States of America

Designed by Jane Byers

Contents

The U.S. Frogmen
of World War II

The U.S. Navy's First True Frogmen

From the deck of the APD *Gilmer*—an old four-stack destroyer converted to use as a troop transport —Lieutenant Commander Draper Kauffman looked out at the vast armada moving westward across the Pacific. Around him were other and far bigger transports, crowded with more than a hundred thousand troops. Battleships, carriers, cruisers, destroyers and tankers spread across the ocean in every direction as far as the eye could see.

It was June, 1944. Somewhere ahead of the fleet lay the Japanese-held island of Saipan, which the American forces planned to invade. And to Lieutenant Commander Kauffman it seemed that the success of the entire invasion might well depend on the work of just 200 naked swimmers, the members of Underwater Demolition Teams 5 and 7. These were the men who, in broad daylight, were scheduled to swim directly toward the beaches, right into the muzzles of enemy guns. There they had to clear away any barriers that might block the

Landing craft head for the beaches to launch the invasion of Saipan.

path of American landing craft.

In all the history of warfare nothing quite like this had ever been tried before. In fact when Kauffman, the senior officer of these demolition teams, had first heard the plan, he could scarcely believe it.

A few months earlier he had been called to Admiral Richmond Kelly Turner's office in Pearl Harbor. On the wall there was a huge map of Saipan. With his forefinger Admiral Turner drew an imaginary line along the western side of the island. "Here," he said, "are the beaches on which we plan to land. And here," he moved his finger slightly to the left, "is a coral reef protecting them. At the north end, this reef is about one mile offshore. Down here, about half a mile."

Kauffman leaned forward, adjusting his glasses to get a better look at the map. He was a tall, sunburned young man, lean now from overwork.

Admiral Turner explained that on the day before the invasion he wanted Kauffman and his men to swim in over the reef, across the lagoon, and up to the beaches. He wanted them to make accurate charts of the depth of the water, and to locate and destroy any underwater obstacles the Japanese might have placed in the lagoon. "We don't want another blunder," he said, "like the one at Tarawa."

Kauffman understood. During the American invasion of Tarawa, hundreds of men had been lost—and the battle itself almost forfeited—because many of the landing boats had been grounded on reefs far out from the beach.

"What time will we go in, sir?" Kauffman asked.

"Nine o'clock."

"Will it be the dark of the moon, or a full moon?"

"It will be 0900—nine o'clock in the morning," Turner answered. "I want you to see what you are doing."

Lieutenant Commander Kauffman looked at Admiral Turner with something close to fear and disbelief in his eyes. Men simply did not swim right up to a fortified enemy beach in broad daylight. "I know what you are thinking," the Admiral said. "But back of you we'll have everything from our battleships to our destroyers pouring fire onto that island. We'll make the Japs keep their heads down so they can't bother you too much . . . I hope."

"Yes, sir," Kauffman said.

He left the Admiral's office and went out into the bright Hawaiian sunlight. Yellow-billed myna birds hopped along the sidewalk in front of him. Flowers bloomed everywhere. The air was filled with the sounds of the harbor: the creak of machinery, the small thunder of air hammers, the

Island Groups in the Pacific

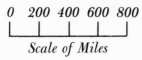

0   200 400 600 800

Scale of Miles

N

W ——|—— E

S

•Midway

OCEAN

•Wake

HAWAIIAN ISLANDS

Kwajalein

MARSHALL ISLANDS

Tarawa

GILBERT ISLANDS

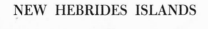

NEW HEBRIDES ISLANDS

voices of workmen and sailors. Across the harbor, alongside Ford Island, Kauffman could see what was left of the battleship *Arizona*. It had been sunk during the Japanese sneak attack on December 7, 1941. Now only a little of the ship still showed above the surface, but on that steel skeleton an American flag flew proudly.

The attack on Saipan would be America's first attempt to crack what Japan considered her inner line of defense. This was a line running almost due south from Japan through the Bonin and Volcano Islands, the Marianas (of which Saipan was one), the Carolines, and on to New Guinea. The Japanese high command was prepared to lose the islands to the east of this line. But the line itself would be defended to the death.

Kauffman thought about this as he walked along the dock. A young man of undeniable courage, Draper Kauffman had gone to Annapolis. But after graduation he failed to receive a commission in the United States Navy because of his poor eyesight. Undaunted, he sought military service abroad.

In the early days of World War II, before the United States entered the conflict, Kauffman drove an ambulance in France. Eventually he was captured by the Germans, then released because he was a noncombatant. Decorated by the French government for his bravery, he lost little time in joining the British navy, where he volunteered for the extremely dangerous job of bomb disposal. Twice he was commended by King George for heroism. When America entered the war he transferred to the United States Navy, which was now pleased to have his services. Once more he volunteered for extra hazardous duty, this time with the newly formed, and as yet almost untested, Underwater Demolition Teams.

At the time of Kauffman's talk with Admiral Turner, in April of 1944, the Underwater Demolition Teams had been training for what they called "sneak and peek" warfare: to slip into enemy waters at night, do what damage was possible, and silently steal away. For the Saipan invasion Admiral Turner was calling for something else altogether.

One tremendous drawback to Turner's plan was immediately apparent. Although Kauffman's men were skilled at destroying mines and blowing up other underwater obstacles, they expected to reach these barriers, or at least come close to them, by boat. Untrained in distance swimming, a UDT (Underwater Demolition Team) man was required to swim no farther than six hundred yards. At Saipan parts of the barrier reef were three times that far offshore. Kauffman wasn't sure that he himself could swim a mile to the beach and a mile back.

Furthermore, his men had no self-contained underwater breathing equipment. So they would have to swim on the surface into the teeth of 20,000 Japanese armed with rifles, machine guns, mortars and artillery.

With luck, Kauffman thought, casualties might be held to fifty percent. With luck—and with training. The lives of his men would depend on their training.

As soon as he returned to Maui, the Hawaiian island where his men were training, Kauffman announced that no UDT man could participate in the coming expedition unless he could swim at least one mile. And he set his men to practicing. They swam in the surf and in the open ocean. They swam during the daylight hours and at night. And always they swam in pairs, the buddy system, so that if one man became exhausted, or if he were wounded, there would be someone close by to help.

Then there was the problem of how to make an accurate chart of the depth of the water inside the lagoon and the exact position of mines and barriers. How could a man swimming under enemy fire know exactly where he was? And how could he keep a record of what he found?

Kauffman discussed this problem with his officers

Lieutenant Commander Draper Kauffman receives a gold star for outstanding heroism during the American invasion of the Marianas.

and enlisted men, and they eventually arrived at a successful solution. Later Kauffman would say, "Practically all the UDT accomplishments were team accomplishments. A great many of our ideas came from the bottom up rather than the top down. These were wonderful men to work with."

11

Together, the officers and men worked out what became known as the "string reconnaissance." A man would take a huge reel of fishing line knotted at twenty-five-yard intervals. After fastening one end of the line to a buoy, he would begin to swim toward the beach, carrying the reel. Each time he reached a knot in the string he would make a sounding and write down the depth and location on a plastic tablet hung around his neck. Since the line from each buoy used a distinctive set of knots, a swimmer could determine his location even at night.

Obviously this was going to take a lot of fishline. Kauffman sent one of his officers to Pearl Harbor to get 150 miles of it. At Pearl Harbor the supply officer looked at the UDT man and shook his head. "I thought we came out here to fight a war," he said. "And you men at Maui are out fishing. What kind of fishing is it where you need 150 miles of line?"

"Japanese fishing," the officer told him, and got his fishing line.

Next Kauffman ordered each man to paint his body and arms with black stripes one foot apart. It was particularly important to know the exact depth in the shallows, since an error of half a foot or so might cause a landing craft to go aground or a tank's engine to drown out in deep water. Painted, a man had only to stand on the bottom and look at his own body to judge the depth within a few inches.

In late May of 1944 the training was completed, and the men boarded APDs for the Saipan invasion. These old destroyers converted to high-speed transports were small and crowded. All the UDT officers had to be quartered with the ship's officers, who already had very little space. Eighty enlisted men were jammed into the forward fireroom, from which the boilers had been removed. Often it was so hot and uncomfortable that the men claimed the ghosts of the old boilers were still at work.

In addition, tons and tons of high explosives were jammed in with the men, making their situation even more unbearable. The explosives would be needed to destroy the reef and the Japanese-built barriers guarding Saipan. A dropped match, a single hit by an enemy shell, might send the whole ship up like a sky rocket.

It was from the deck of one of these converted destroyers that Lieutenant Commander Kauffman looked at the surrounding fleet and pondered what lay ahead.

Early on the morning of June 14, the low mountains of Saipan began to loom out of the ocean. There was little wind. A small surf broke across the coral reef, lapping gently at the white sand beaches. Against the sunrise sky the blue lagoon and the lush green hills looked very beautiful and very peaceful. But the men lining up on the decks of the APDs knew that for some of them death was hidden under the beauty.

Several miles offshore most of the warships turned parallel to the island, but the *Gilmer* and the *Brooks*, carrying UDTs 5 and 7, kept going in closer. As they approached the island the other ships began to fire over their heads. The shells whistled past and then exploded with flashes of fire and smoke on the soft green island. But from Saipan there was no return fire. In fact there was no sign of life.

Two miles offshore, a mile outside the barrier reef, the APDs stopped and the UDT men, carrying diving masks, began to climb over the side into small boats. They were a weird-looking lot, with their bodies ringed by black stripes. Besides swimming trunks, they wore tennis shoes; and a few had kneepads for climbing over the coral reef. Plastic pads dangled from their necks, and the men carried balsa-wood floats for marking mines and barriers.

Suddenly, without warning, the sea shot skyward all around them. There was the crash of falling shells. Japanese artillery on the island had opened fire. The very first burst took in the APDs. On the *Gilmer* two men were wounded. Behind her the battleship *California* took a direct hit.

The APDs turned away from the island. But the small boats, loaded with the UDT men, headed straight toward it.

The Japanese artillery and mortars began to concentrate on these small boats. One took an immediate hit, which wounded one man and killed another. Around the other boats shells exploded continually. But the small craft continued to speed closer and closer to the reef. Along the reef were various colored pennants, placed there by the Japanese as range markers for their guns. The closer the boats got to the reef, the more accurate the enemy's fire became.

A hundred yards off the reef the boats turned parallel to it. The UDT men climbed over the rail onto the rubber rafts fastened to the sides of the boats. Upon command, at every fifty yards, two men rolled from the rafts into the water.

Now they were on their own, alone in the sea.

Swimming like porpoises—under water and up for breath and under water again—they approached the reef. By this time it was practically a wall of exploding mortar fire. The men dived and checked the depth and contour on the ocean side. Then, swimming, crawling, they crossed the reef into the lagoon and headed toward the beach itself. One man of each pair carried the reel and fishline for checking distance. This man swam directly toward an assigned point on the beach. Meanwhile his buddy swam zigzag around him, looking for mines and other obstacles the Japanese might have planted.

Kauffman's plan had called for officers to go ahead of the swimmers on "flying mattresses." These were rubber rafts propelled by small electric motors. It was hoped that the men on the mattresses could help the swimmers keep straight, accurate lines. Quickly, however, it became obvious the Japanese were concentrating their fire on the mattresses. Three were sunk almost before they got started, though not a man on them was wounded. But on another raft Robert Christiansen, one of the most popular men on Team 5, was killed.

Kauffman himself was on a flying mattress out in front. It was soon shot full of holes, but he clung to it and to his walkie-talkie radio. The radio was supposed to keep him in touch with the small boats outside the reef and the ships beyond. By using the walkie-talkie, he could direct the ships' fire and give orders. He still wore his glasses, taped on so they would not come off when he had to swim. With him was a sailor named Alex Paige. Paige was called Kauffman's "Seeing Eye" because he was far-sighted. But he was also color-blind. He would see things at a distance and describe them to the Commander. If Kauffman could see the objects, he would in turn tell Paige their color.

Yet even when his glasses were splashed with salt water, Kauffman could see enough to know his men were doing their job. "Every single man," he reported later, "was calmly and slowly continuing his search and marking his slate with stuff dropping all around. They didn't appear one tenth as scared as I was. I would not have been so amazed if ninety percent of the men had done so well, but to have a cold one hundred percent go in through the rain of fire was almost unbelievable." Later the team's official historian would write that the men themselves admitted afterward "they were as far from being calm as they had ever been in their lives."

Calm or not, they kept swimming toward the beach, checking the depth of the lagoon and looking for mines.

As the UDT men drew closer, Japanese snipers and machine guns joined the mortar fire. One man was wounded, then another and another. At least half a dozen suffered internal injuries from nearby mortar bursts. One man was blown completely clear of the water by a shell exploding under him, but he kept up his swimming stroke.

Three hundred yards off the beach Kauffman

anchored his mattress, which was still afloat, though full of holes. The time was now ten o'clock. During this final approach to the beach the bombarding ships moved their fire inland to avoid the risk of killing their own swimmers. Planes from the carriers were scheduled to come in and strafe the beach to keep the Japanese down.

But no planes were visible. Kauffman called for them on his radio, but received no answer. Something had gone wrong. The men were swimming in, closer and closer, without protective fire. The Japanese began to stand up in their foxholes along the beach and shoot directly at the swimmers, who were now sometimes less than thirty yards away. Later, when it was all over, Kauffman would say jokingly, "Luckily, the Japs are poor shots. But it's bad for the swimmers' morale to see them standing up taking aim this close."

Still the swimmers went on, staying under water as much as possible, coming up to catch a fast breath and then dive again. They swam closer and closer, until the water was so shallow they could no longer swim. As soon as they had made certain that the landing craft and tanks would be able to reach the beach, they turned and headed back toward the reef and the open sea beyond.

But the job was not yet over. As the men

With the help of his teammate, a UDT man climbs aboard a raft after completing a mission.

clambered over the reef, the small boats came in to pick them up. To accomplish this the boats had to stop dead in the water, while the mortar fire was concentrated on them. There were more hits, and more men were wounded.

Finally all but two of the men were picked up. These two could not be found. Reluctantly Kauffman had to give orders for the last boat to turn away and abandon the search. Then came word that a cruiser had sighted two men clinging to a buoy a mile and a half from where the teams had swum in. Kauffman's boat headed for the buoy. Here they found gunner's mates A. H. Root and R. E. Heil. Heil had been wounded on the way in. His swim buddy had bandaged the wound, using the waterproof first-aid kit they carried. Then leaving Heil behind, Root had finished his assignment. On the way back he had picked up the wounded man and towed him to the buoy, holding him afloat until the boat came after them.

Back on shipboard the UDT officers worked all night preparing charts of the reef and lagoon. They had learned there were no mines or man-made barriers. But they had also learned that in places the lagoon was deeper than aerial photographs indicated. If tanks had tried to cross in these places, they would have been put out of commission. The UDT men drew maps to show where the tanks could cross safely.

The next day the marines stormed ashore without the terrible casualties they had suffered at Tarawa.

Another job still remained for the UDT men. With

Frogmen aboard a landing craft approach the Saipan beaches, where exploding shells form a wall of smoke and fire.

the marines battling desperately ashore, it was necessary to blow a channel through the reef so that larger craft could bring in additional troops and supplies. Wearing swim trunks and mask, Kauffman went ashore to ask the beach commander where he wanted the channel. A marine, crouched in a foxhole firing at the Japanese hidden in the green foliage ahead, turned and saw Kauffman.

"Now I've seen everything!" he shouted. "We haven't even got the island secure and the tourists are

UDT men load their raft for an expedition off the shores of Saipan.

already here!"

But there was no time yet for laughter. In the next 2 days the UDT men used 105,000 pounds of explosives to blast a path 250 yards long, 30 yards wide and 6 feet deep through the reef and lagoon. Men and supplies poured safely in through this channel until the island was secure.

After the invasion Admiral Turner asked Commander Kauffman to name the UDT men who he felt should be given medals. Kauffman replied that he could not do this. There had been no individual heroes, he said. Every man in both teams had done his duty; every man had carried out the job assigned to him. All had been equally brave. If any medals were to be given, Kauffman said, they should be given to the teams as a whole. Then each man would receive the same award.

At Saipan Teams 5 and 7 each lost one man killed and a number of wounded. But they saved the lives of thousands. As the United States pushed steadily toward Japan, the Navy "frogmen" would play an important part in every invasion.

Frogmen
of Other Countries

The individual swimmer has played a part in warfare from the earliest times. More than 2,000 years ago the Athenians used free-swimming divers to destroy barricades placed across the harbor of Syracuse. Alexander the Great used divers in the same way during the siege of Tyre. In A.D. 1332 a man named Ibn Battuta wrote about a Turkish sultan, Ghazi Chelebi, who "was a brave and an audacious man with a peculiar capacity for swimming under water. He used to swim out with his war vessels to fight the Greeks, and when the fleets met and everyone was occupied with the fighting, he would dive under the water carrying an iron tool with which he pierced the enemy's ships and they knew nothing about it until all at once they sank."

There is, however, no need to go back to Ghazi Chelebi to learn what the courage and skill of the individual diver can accomplish. Toward the end of World War I two Italian naval officers named Raffaele Paolucci and Raffael Rossetti invented a motor-

Two frogmen "ride horseback" on an Italian World War II human torpedo.

driven torpedo with a detachable warhead. One dark night they rode it, like two seagoing cowboys, into the harbor at Pola, Austria. They dragged and pushed and tugged the torpedo over eight different nets and barriers until they reached the Austrian battleship *Viribus Unitis*. After detaching the warhead from the nose of the torpedo, they dived and fastened it to the bottom of the battleship. Before they could escape from the harbor, they were captured. But the timing device on the warhead had already been set. It exploded and sank the battleship.

Early in World War II the Italians invented an improved version of Rossetti and Paolucci's torpedo. This one, with two men riding it like a horse, would run either on the surface or under water. The men breathed pure oxygen from a kind of aqualung. Oxygen taken at depths of more than thirty feet will sometimes act like a deadly poison. Taken at any depth by a man who is swimming and breathing hard, oxygen can be extremely dangerous. Yet with only their crude aqualung and new torpedo, the Italians accomplished some remarkable feats.

They began by attacking ships docked at Gibraltar, a British crown colony on the Mediterranean Sea. Riding their torpedoes into the harbor at night, they attached limpets—magnetic mines equipped with a time fuse—to the bottoms of ships. The British

countered by developing their own teams of frogmen, who swam under the ships in the harbor and
searched for mines. On one occasion a British and
an Italian frogman fought hand to hand beneath the
bottom of a ship. British frogmen, working out of
midget submarines, also attacked and sank both
German and Japanese warships. And in the icy fiords
of Norway some underground Norwegian resistance
fighters became frogmen. Frequently they managed
to fasten limpets to the bottoms of German ships and
sink them.

It was the Italians, however, who were to use the
horseback-torpedo in one of the most amazing
episodes of the war.

It happened this way.

In November, 1941, before America's entrance into
the war, British resources were strained to the limit.
Part of the British fleet was tied down in the North
Sea to guard against raids by the German battleship
Tirpitz, the most powerful warship in the world at
that time. Another part of Britain's fleet had been
sent to the Far East, where it was feared the Japanese
might join the war at any moment. And in North
Africa, British ground troops were fighting desperately against strong German and Italian forces. Here
it seemed very likely that whoever controlled the
Mediterranean Sea and could bring in reinforcements

with the smallest loss would win. Certainly a victory in North Africa would influence the whole course of the war.

At this crucial point German submarines in the Mediterranean sank the British aircraft carrier *Ark Royal* and, not quite two weeks later, the battleship *Barham*. This left the British with only two battleships, the *Queen Elizabeth* and the *Valiant*, plus some smaller craft, to oppose the entire Italian fleet in the Mediterranean. To make sure the two battleships remained safe until needed in an emergency, the British ordered them to Alexandria Harbor in Egypt. There they were surrounded by every known protective device.

Italian aircraft spotted the ships but could not bomb them because of massed anti-aircraft batteries. In fact it seemed that nothing could possibly reach the two powerful British ships. There were, however, a few men in the Italian navy, in a unit called the Tenth Light Flotilla, who thought they could do it. These were the Italian frogmen who rode horseback on the torpedoes they called "Pigs."

One night early in December, 1941, about two weeks after the sinking of the *Barham*, six Italian frogmen boarded the submarine *Scire* and set out to destroy the two giant British battleships. With their three pigs fastened to the deck of the submarine, they traveled across the Mediterranean. Outside Alexandria, for a distance of twenty miles or more, the British had sown mine fields. Carefully, far below the surface, the *Scire* nosed her way through the mines. The submarine had to take the frogmen as close as possible to the harbor because the pigs, operated by electric motors, could run for only a few miles.

At 6:40 P.M. on December 18, the *Scire* reached her destination, exactly one and three-tenths miles from the lighthouse at the western end of Alexandria Harbor. She lay there submerged until night had fallen. Then she rose until her deck was close to the surface. The frogmen, wearing rubber suits, masks and oxygen lungs, climbed up the ladders and onto the submerged deck. Working under water they released the pigs from their cylinders and, with two men on each pig, rode off into the night. The submarine turned back toward Italy.

The frogmen were under the command of Lieutenant Luigi Durand de la Penne. A large, easygoing blond man, he had spent most of the trip across the Mediterranean resting and eating fruit cake. He was going to have need of all his strength and energy before this night was over.

Submerged so that only the heads of the six riders were above the surface, the three pigs moved slowly

An aerial view of the British naval base at Alexandria, July, 1942.

toward the shore. The night was inky dark; the city of Alexandria was blacked out, but some of the tallest buildings showed dimly against the sky. As the men neared the long breakwater that formed the outer edge of the harbor, they turned their pigs toward the entrance to the harbor. The frogmen were so close they could see men on the pier and even hear them talking. One man carried a lantern, and its rays gleamed on the water, almost lighting up the six dark heads as they moved slowly past. De la Penne's rubber suit was leaking, and the water was icy cold. He wondered that the men on the pier did not hear his teeth chattering.

Just ahead there was a sudden explosion. The resulting concussion struck the frogmen like a hammer blow. Then came another explosion, and a few minutes later still another. Ahead of them, the frogmen saw a British torpedo boat, low against the water, dropping depth charges. Since the British were well acquainted with the Italian pigs from their use at Gibraltar, they were protecting the harbor against just such an attack at Alexandria. (They didn't, however, suspect that one was just about to take place.)

The torpedo boat moved away. Now the frogmen were opposite the harbor entrance, which they knew was protected by a gigantic anti-submarine net. They had to find the net and get their pigs over or under it without discovery.

Suddenly a destroyer loomed up behind them, almost smashing into the torpedo ridden by de la Penne. The wake from the destroyer washed one of the other pigs against the pier, but fortunately did not damage it. De la Penne realized the anti-submarine net had been lowered to let the destroyer pass through. Quickly he and his men followed.

Inside the harbor, the pigs separated, each one heading for its own objective.

De la Penne's job was to sink the battleship *Valiant*. He had studied aerial photographs of the harbor and knew exactly where to find her. But he was still a hundred feet from the ship when his pig nosed into another steel net.

The frogman riding with de la Penne was named Bianchi. The two of them climbed off their iron mount and, by pushing and pulling, tried to roll it over the net. They could hear the British sailors talking on the ship, so they knew that any noise could be easily overheard. And any big splash might even be seen.

Somehow they got the torpedo over the net and mounted it again. They were breathing hard now. De la Penne started the motor and nosed the torpedo downward. As the water closed over their heads, de la Penne steered by the luminous dial of his wrist compass.

They were within a few feet of the ship—de la Penne's outstretched hand had actually touched it— when the pig abruptly swerved off course and began to dive. It refused to respond to the rudder, and plunged to the bottom in fifty feet of water.

De la Penne was trying to discover what had gone wrong with the mechanism when he suddenly realized Bianchi was missing. The Lieutenant swam to the surface. The giant battleship loomed almost directly overhead, but there was no sign of Bianchi. Either he was lost in the darkness or had been overcome by oxygen poisoning. Since there was no time to search for him, de la Penne dived down into the water again. He found the torpedo and tried to start the motor, but it would not work. A piece of wire cable had tangled in the propeller.

There was nothing to do except try to drag the torpedo by brute force to a position directly under the ship. The Lieutenant went to work. He was below the safe depth for oxygen, and working with all his strength, but he did not pause. Inch by inch he moved the torpedo. Mud stirred up from the harbor bottom fogged his mask so he could no longer read his compass. But he could hear sounds from inside the ship, particularly the throbbing of a pump, and he used those as a guide.

It took him forty minutes to get the torpedo into position. By the time he finally felt the hull of the ship above him, he was almost unconscious. With the last of his strength he set the time fuse to go off at six o'clock, the time designated in his orders. Then he swam slowly to the surface, where he managed to strip off his mask and gulp in the fresh air. Revived, he began to swim wearily toward shore.

Suddenly a searchlight swept across him, then swept back and caught him in its beam. A burst of machine-gun fire slashed the water ahead of him. He turned and swam back to the *Valiant*. Exhausted, he managed to climb onto her mooring buoy.

Here he found Bianchi, who had fainted when the torpedo dived. Floating to the surface, he had regained consciousness and climbed onto the buoy without knowing just where he was.

Both men were picked up and taken by motorboat to the dock, where they were questioned. When they refused to talk they were taken back to the very ship they had mined, and locked in a small cabin below decks.

Here they sat until ten minutes before the time set for the explosion. At this point de la Penne asked to see the commanding officer. He told him the ship was mined and there was no possible way to save it, but the crew could be saved if they were sent ashore immediately. The *Valiant's* captain asked where the mine was placed. When the Italian officer refused to say, he was once more taken below decks. From there he could hear the ship's siren and the crew being ordered ashore.

The Lieutenant's watch showed one minute of six. Then six. Then a minute after. He began to wonder if something had gone wrong with the mine, if all his backbreaking work was in vain. At the same time he wondered if there would be any way to save his own life if the *Valiant* sank.

Suddenly the great ship shuddered under the impact of a tremendous explosion. In de la Penne's cabin, objects crashed violently against the bulkheads and the door flew open. The Lieutenant rushed up on deck. In the early morning light he looked around for the *Queen Elizabeth,* the second target. Just as he located her, the ship leaped in the water. Frag-

Repairs are begun on the Valiant *following the attack by Italian frogmen of the Tenth Light Flotilla.*

More than twenty years after his successful attack on the Valiant, *Luigi Durand de la Penne exhibits a manometer from one of the Italian "pigs" on which he served.*

ments of iron and oil and flame shot skyward. A moment later, across the harbor, a tanker exploded. All three of the pigs had reached their targets.

The tanker had been blown up in the hope that flames from the burning oil would spread across the harbor and set all the ships and docks afire. But this fire did not materialize. Even so, six men had put two battleships and a tanker out of commission. Britain was left without a single workable battleship in the Mediterranean whereas the Italians had five. At this moment they were in absolute control of the Mediterranean Sea.

Strangely, the Italian navy did not take advantage of the situation. For one thing, they were not sure the British battleships were useless. All the frogmen had been captured, so they could not report what they had done. Also, in the comparatively shallow water of the harbor, the ships had not sunk completely but had only settled on the bottom. Aerial photos showed them still there, obviously damaged but possibly still useful. So the Italian and German high commands hesitated. Before they could decide what to do, new British ships—along with ships from the United States, which had entered the war following the Japanese attack on Pearl Harbor—arrived in the Mediterranean to change the situation.

Nothing, however, could take away from the gallantry, the almost incredible accomplishment of the six Italian frogmen. They had invaded an enemy harbor and, without the loss of a single life, destroyed the backbone of Great Britain's Mediterranean fleet.

Tarawa
and Kwajalein

Despite the accomplishments of de la Penne and other Italian, British and Norwegian frogmen, the United States Navy was slow in developing its own teams of underwater swimmers. Prior to the invasion of Saipan, the Americans tended to emphasize mechanical gadgets such as robot boats with radio controls. Some of these proved of value. Yet gradually it became clear that, no matter how complex war might be, machines could not replace the eyes and brain and courage of the individual human being.

This lesson was learned the hard way during the terrible invasion of Tarawa.

In November of 1943, American forces were about to begin the long, hard fight across the Central Pacific toward Japan. The first step was to be the low, barren atoll of Tarawa in the Gilbert Islands.

A cluster of small islands surrounded by coral reefs, the Tarawa atoll is shaped like a V lying on its side. The little island which forms the tip of its lower

On ravaged Tarawa two marines man a machine gun.

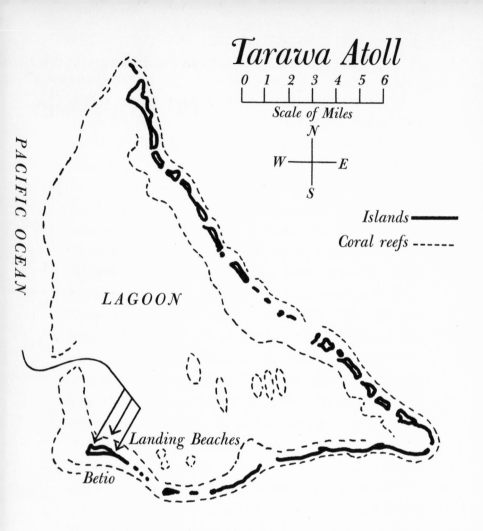

Tarawa Atoll

0 1 2 3 4 5 6

Scale of Miles

N
W —+— E
S

Islands ———
Coral reefs - - - - -

PACIFIC OCEAN

LAGOON

Landing Beaches

Betio

arm is named Betio. Here the Japanese concentrated most of their defenses. To reach the enemy on Betio, boats and men would have to cross a coral reef, as well as several hundred yards of shallow water between the reef and the island.

In planning the invasion the American commanders took what must have seemed to them to be every possible precaution. Not much was known about Tarawa. The only oceanographic survey had been made in 1841, a hundred and two years earlier. In the meantime the surrounding coral reefs had been growing. So a submarine was sent to prowl around as close as possible to the atoll and make soundings. Since the submarine could not explore the shallow water, airplanes flew overhead and took thousands of photographs. But these could not show the exact depth of the water over the reefs. Men were found who had traded with the islands just before the war, but unfortunately they had made no detailed charts. It was generally believed, however, that the water over the reef was about five feet deep—deep enough to allow the passage of landing craft.

For days before the invasion the atoll was bombed and shelled. As one officer reported later, "The island was so covered with bomb and shell fragments a man couldn't walk without stepping on them." It seemed impossible that any Japanese could have survived such a bombardment.

Despite all these precautions, the Betio landing went badly. The Japanese had converted the entire island into a fort. There were artillery emplacements everywhere, dug deep into the ground, roofed over

41

by concrete and sand, and hidden beneath the palms. These emplacements were connected by trenches and underground tunnels. There were hundreds of cannon, mortar and machine guns trained to sweep the beach and the lagoon. Protected and hidden, these had been only partially knocked out by the bombardment.

To make matters far worse, the water over the reef was not as deep as expected. Landing craft got hung

A *section of the devastated Tarawa lagoon shortly after the American invasion forces had moved on.*

up, and Japanese artillery fire zeroed in on them. Men and tanks had to be discharged there instead of on or close to the beach. Waddling through the lagoon, some of the tanks ran into deep water and sank or had their motors drowned out. Men had to wade through waist-deep water, sometimes for as much as a mile and a half, exposed to intense fire. Losses were dreadful and for many hours the outcome hung in doubt. Finally enough marines got

43

ashore to crush the enemy. But almost one-third of all the men landed that day were killed or wounded —most of them before they even reached the beach.

Terrible Tarawa, as it was called, made clear the fact that an offshore reef could be a very effective barrier against invasion, particularly if everything about the reef and the water depth was not known. But at this time, seven months before the invasion of Saipan, the United States Navy had no organization trained to make such a survey. The groups designed to destroy beach defenses were called Naval Combat Demolition Units. Although the men were experts in the use of explosives, they were supposed to reach their objectives by boats and not by swimming. After Tarawa these units were reorganized, and for the first time the word "Underwater" appeared in their title. The Naval Combat Demolition Units became Underwater Demolition Teams, and swimming began to be stressed in their training.

Even so, swimming remained relatively unimportant with the first UDTs. Mechanical gadgets were invented to blast the reefs. Most of these inventions were boats of various kinds, loaded with explosives and steered by radio. The UDT men were supposed to ride them fairly close to the reefs, then transfer to other boats. From these they could steer the explosive-laden craft to the reef by radio and explode them. For the invasion of Kwajalein, a few hundred miles northwest of Tarawa, many of these boats were taken along.

They didn't work. Some sank before they reached the reef; others exploded in the wrong places. A few actually turned and went in the opposite direction— toward the American fleet and the troops coming in to land.

Nevertheless, it was at Kwajalein, two months after the fierce Tarawa fighting, that the UDTs took their first long step toward becoming a true frogman force. On the day before the invasion, men from UDT were ordered to go as close to the reef as possible in four small boats. They were to search for mines, learn how the reef was shaped and investigate the depth of the tide there. The shape of the reef was important because this would determine whether or not amphibious craft, called alligators or amtracks, could crawl over the reef, even if the water was too shallow for them to float over it.

It was hoped that gunfire from the offshore fleet would keep most of the Japanese snipers and machine gunners under cover. And the Japanese commander would probably not want to expose the hidden positions of his big guns by firing them at the four little landing craft to be used for the survey. But how much could the UDT men actually learn about the reef as long as they remained in their boats?

Ensign Lew Luehrs and Chief Bill Acheson, who were to go together in one boat, discussed the mission. Luehrs thought they could get closer to the reef by swimming than by boat. And they would also be able to learn more. Acheson agreed.

So when they climbed into the landing craft that was to take them to the reef, they wore bathing trunks under their uniforms. They had not, however, said anything about this to the other men for fear of being laughed at.

Only a few enemy shells were fired at the boats, and none of these came close. In fact the reef itself, as they approached, seemed more dangerous than the Japanese shells. It was covered with coral heads, which would sink any boat that struck them. The coxswain of the landing craft did not want to come too close.

Luehrs said, "What do you think, Chief?"

"I'm for it," Acheson said.

The two UDT men stripped off their uniforms and dived over the side of the landing craft. After reaching the reef, they carefully made their way along it, searching for mines. Then they swam between the coral heads and searched the other side. Luehrs and Acheson were in the water for forty-five minutes before returning to their boat.

When they reached the ship, they were taken immediately to Admiral Turner, who was in command of the invasion. They reported they had found no mines, but that the numerous coral heads would make crossing the reef dangerous if not impossible for regular boats. On the other hand, they believed amtracks could cross it safely.

The landing took place in amtracks, with only moderate losses.

Young Lew Luehrs and Bill Acheson had proved that sometimes a brave man swimming naked in the sea could be of more value than the most elaborate mechanical devices.

The Normandy Invasion

Five months after Kwajalein and nine days before the invasion of Saipan, the great Normandy landings took place on the coast of France. The date was June 6, 1944. The tremendous invasion force, under the command of General Dwight · D. Eisenhower, was based in Great Britain and composed not only of English and American forces but of units from other Allies as well.

Across the English Channel, along the Normandy coast, where the armies would land, there were no hidden coral reefs. There was, however, a twenty-five-foot tide that would rise at the rate of one foot every eight minutes and rush across the beach just about as fast as a man might walk. Beyond the beach, low walls barred the way in some places; in others there were sheer cliffs with artillery emplacements on top. And the beaches themselves were covered by the most formidable man-made barriers ever erected.

For over a year the German dictator, Adolf Hitler,

A deserted Nazi gun emplacement overlooking a section of the Normandy coast.

had been preparing for an Allied invasion on the French coast. He had kept more than a half-million men—both soldiers and civilians—busy building defenses. Already the Allies had driven the Germans out of North Africa; they had made landings in Sicily and Italy. But Hitler was certain that the final blow, the greatest of all, would come straight across the English Channel against the French coast. On the success or failure of this invasion attempt might turn the outcome of the whole European war. Hitler, as well as the Allies, realized its importance. Late in the fall of 1943 he sent Field Marshal Erwin Rommel, his most famous general, to take charge of the Normandy coastal defenses and improve them.

From the time he arrived at his new job Rommel worked tirelessly. Carrying a pencil and paper, he would walk up and down the beaches, designing new death traps for boats and men. He worked his soldiers day and night building these fortifications. When one of his officers complained that his men were getting no rest, Rommel turned on him furiously. "Had they rather be tired or dead?" he demanded.

Some of the German generals did not believe in the beach defenses. They thought the best strategy was to hold most of their troops, particularly the armored divisions, well back from the coast, out of range of the Allied naval bombardment. Then after the American and British troops had come ashore, the Germans would counterattack and drive them back into the sea. Rommel disagreed. Pointing to the water's edge he told his officers, "There is where the battle is going to be won or lost. Right there."

Up and down the shoreline Rommel built reinforced concrete bunkers from which cannon and machine guns and mortars could sweep both the beaches and the sea. And in front of the bunkers, on the beaches themselves, the Germans built more than a half-million obstacles designed to wreck any kind of boat that touched them. Some of these were of steel, some of concrete. Others were made with wood, and practically all were topped by mines that would explode on touch. Between these obstacles, all across the beaches, the Nazis sowed mines like seeds—more than five million of them!

These were the death traps the British and American demolition units would have to destroy if the great invasion was to be a success.

Because of the tremendous tides which sweep the English Channel along the French coast, practically all of Rommel's obstacles were above water at low tide, but flooded at high tide. The Allies planned to have their powerful armada arrive offshore before daylight, when the tide was going out. From a

(Left) A German beach obstacle topped by an explosive teller mine. (Below) An aerial view of the death traps erected by the Nazis along the French coast.

starting point about five miles off the beach, a wave of swimming tanks would lead the way, reaching the shore at dead low tide. One minute later a thin line of specially trained infantry would arrive to clean up any German snipers near the water. Right on the heels of the line of infantry would come the Navy demolition men and Army engineers. Working on dry land, just ahead of the advancing tide, they would blow gaps through the beach defenses so that all the following boatloads of men, tanks and supplies could come ashore safely.

It was almost a split-second schedule. The demolitioneers were given just twenty-seven minutes in which to destroy the defenses the Germans had been building for more than a year.

As is usual with gigantic plans, not everything went according to schedule.

The water was rough—too rough for the swimming tanks. Out of twenty-nine tanks in one group, twenty-seven floundered and sank without reaching the shore. A strong wind and tide carried other landing craft off their course. Many of them hit the beach a mile or more from where they should have been. Some arrived late, and others were early. In places the demolition men, armed only with huge piles of explosives, arrived on shore ahead of the tanks and infantry assigned to protect them.

Nor had all the carefully hidden German guns on the shore been knocked out by the pre-invasion bombardment. The long line of approaching boats was still a half-mile offshore when these guns opened up with deadly accuracy. One landing craft carrying demolitioneers took a direct hit. All the explosives piled aboard went off in a gigantic flash, hurling fragments of men and machinery high into the sky. Another boat dropped its debarking ramp directly onto a mine, while a third opened its ramp just in time for a German shell to hurtle directly into the boat in the midst of the massed men and explosives.

But the men who survived kept going. Chief Gunner's Mate Bill Freeman was in command of Demolition Unit 2. Originally he was not supposed to be the commanding officer, but a last-minute promotion of his immediate superior left him in charge of the naval unit working alongside a unit from the army. Freeman's landing craft dropped its ramp just off the beach at exactly the right time, 6:33 A.M., three minutes after the first wave of tanks should have landed. But the tanks and protecting infantry were late; Freeman and his demolitioneers were the first men on the beach.

As artillery, mortar and machine-gun fire rained around them, they waded toward the first row of obstacles, carrying their explosives in small waterproof canvas bags called Hagensen packs. While some tied the Hagensen packs to the obstacles, others remained by the landing craft to unload the extra explosives onto a rubber raft. Gunfire hit the raft and sank it. Then the men who had been loading it were cut down.

But on the beach Chief Freeman and his men continued their work. When the first line of obstacles was loaded with Hagensen packs, a sailor rushed up and down tying them together with detonating cord. Then Freeman touched it off. There was a tremendous roar as the explosives blew a fifty-yard gap in the first row of beach defenses. But ahead were four more rows, and the German fire was becoming even fiercer.

In the face of this mounting opposition, Freeman led his men to the new row of obstacles. By now some of the tanks that should have been ahead of him were just landing. This caused tremendous confusion. Instead of passing the demolitioneers and advancing toward the enemy positions, the tanks stayed where they were at the water's edge, firing over the demolition unit. When Freeman saw that his men were caught between two fires, he shouted and waved at the tanks to advance. Slowly they moved ahead.

When the second row of obstacles was ready to be

ignited, a new delay occurred. The troops that should have been on the beach ahead of the demolitioneers had only just landed. Confronted by the terrific German fire, many of the men had frozen with terror. They would not advance across the beach. Some of them had taken shelter directly behind and under the obstacles that were ready to be exploded.

Freeman ran among the terrified soldiers, ordering them to move ahead. Many refused, too petrified to move.

"All right!" Freeman shouted. "In one minute I'm

Encountering heavy enemy fire, American soldiers at Omaha Beach take cover behind obstacles.

going to blow up this part of the beach. If you go ahead, you've got a chance. But anybody who stays here is going to be killed!"

The soldiers began to advance.

Behind the demolitioneers the tide was coming in, faster and faster. Already the water was ankle deep around the obstacles to be blown up. Soon it was calf deep. But finally the section of beach was cleared and Freeman set off the blast that destroyed the second row of obstacles. Then he and his men moved on to the third, then the fourth row.

Because the demolitioneers were expected to work ahead of the tide, they had come ashore fully dressed in special uniforms impregnated against mustard gas, if the Germans should use it. But now some of the men had to wade and swim back through the rising water to put floating markers along the sides of the gap they had blown through the obstacles. The markers would enable the assault boats to find a safe route into the beach. Once this job was completed, the men struggled ashore again.

Eventually Freeman and what was left of his demolition unit took shelter behind a low wall. The Chief had been slightly wounded, but he took no notice of this. (Later, he would not even mention it in his report.) The more seriously wounded were made as comfortable as possible on inflated life belts and given emergency first-aid treatment.

When the tide began to withdraw, Chief Freeman rounded up those men in his unit who were still able to work. Collecting more explosives from Army engineers, he once again led his men onto the open beach to follow the outgoing tide. Then they blew a wider gap through the defenses.

For a long time the battle at bloody Omaha Beach hung in doubt. At one point that morning, General Omar Bradley, commander of the American ground forces, seriously considered withdrawing his men. But eventually the Allied troops began to push ahead.

After the battle Chief Freeman was made a commissioned officer and awarded a gold star in lieu of a second Navy Cross. (He had already won one Navy Cross in North Africa.) The citation read:

For extraordinary heroism as Leader of Naval Combat Demolition Unit TWO, attached to the ELEVENTH Amphibious Force during the assault on the coast of France, June 6, 1944. Braving heavy German artillery and small arms fire, Lieutenant Junior Grade, (then Chief Gunners Mate) Freeman led his crew on to the assault beaches at H-hour plus three minutes in an attempt to blow a fifty yard gap through the formidable beach obstacles. Although seven of the twelve-man unit were killed or wounded by the terrific gunfire, he succeeded in accomplishing this perilous and vital mission. Heedless of his own safety, he repeatedly exposed himself to intense gunfire to recover wounded personnel and bring them to a place of comparative safety. By his inspiring leadership, aggressive fighting spirit and unwavering devotion to duty, Lieutenant Junior Grade, Freeman contributed directly to the success of his vital operations and upheld the highest traditions of the United States Naval service.

Chief Bill Freeman was not the only hero among the Navy's demolitioneers that day. All up and down the bloody Omaha and Utah beaches men worked bravely in order to save the lives of the others who had to follow them ashore. Of the 175 Naval Combat Demolitioneers in the Omaha Beach invasion, 31 were killed and 60 wounded. In other words, fifty-two percent of the men were casualties.

The Normandy invasion was the last major invasion in which the demolitioneers were not swimmers.

Tinian and Guam

Eight days after the Normandy landings came the invasion of Saipan on the other side of the world. There Lieutenant Commander Draper Kauffman and his demolitioneers became the first true American underwater frogmen.

The successful landing on Saipan was the first crack in Japan's inner line of defense. But before the island base could be fully utilized, two nearby islands—Tinian and Guam—had to be captured. Both of these islands were better suited than Saipan for large airfields. And once they were in American hands, the Army's new B-29 Superfortresses could use them as bases from which to strike directly at the Japanese homeland.

While the fighting continued on Saipan, UDT men began to explore the beaches of the other two islands. Teams 3, 4 and 6 were sent to Guam, while Teams 5 and 7, the same teams that had worked on Saipan, were assigned to Tinian.

Aerial photographs showed that there were several

Prior to the American landings, the guns of a U.S. Navy cruiser bombard Guam.

beaches on Tinian. On the southwestern side of the island, near the town of Tinian, there was a particularly long, wide, beautiful beach that looked like a perfect place for a landing. The Japanese obviously thought so too, because the aerial photographs revealed heavy concentrations of artillery on the cliffs at each end of the beach. And the closeness of the town to the beach meant that the marines would be engaged in door-to-door street fighting almost as soon as they landed. Marine General H. M. Smith, who was in charge of the invasion, did not want to land on this beach if he could avoid it.

On the northeastern side of Tinian there was another fair-sized beach, but it too was heavily fortified. Then on the northwestern side of the island, there were two very small beaches separated by a cliff. One was only about sixty yards wide; the other was about a hundred yards wide. General Smith—whose troops called him "Howlin' Mad" Smith because of his temper—had an idea the Japanese might have considered these beaches too small for a landing and thus have neglected to fortify them. But because of the heavy tropical growth right behind them, it was impossible to obtain adequate information from the air. Nor did aerial photographs show if there were any exits from these beaches to the high plateau land that formed most of the interior of

An aerial photograph of the northern tip of Tinian.

the island. If the beaches were fortified, and without proper exits, a landing in that area would be mass suicide.

There was just one way to tell. General Smith sent UDT 5 under Lieutenant Commander Kauffman to find out. A Marine unit under Lieutenant Leo Shinn was to go with them. The marines were to explore the exits from the beaches, while the UDT men searched the approaches and the beach area itself for mines and traps. The reconnaissance was to be performed as secretly as possible. If the beaches were unfortified, General Smith did not want to alert the Japanese to the fact that this area of the island was under consideration for an invasion.

On the night of the exploratory expedition there was a full moon, concealed at times by small, dark clouds. Sliding in and out of the moonlight, the APD *Gilmer* came from behind Saipan and moved as close as possible to Tinian. Then she stopped and put over the small boats that would carry the men to within swimming distance of the beaches.

At this point things started to go wrong. The *Gilmer* was supposed to guide the small boats toward their destinations by radio and radar, but suddenly the radar went bad. At the same time a low fog began forming near the water, and from the boats it was impossible to see the blacked-out island ahead.

Also, though no one yet knew it, the current that was supposed to be moving southward along the beaches was actually going north.

In the foggy darkness the small boats had to guess at their distance from shore. And when the swimmers were in the water, guiding themselves by their wrist compasses, they soon lost all contact with one another.

Abruptly one UDT man saw something dark just ahead of him. For an instant he thought it was a block of wood; then he saw a slight splash and knew it was another swimmer. But the man seemed to be coming toward him instead of swimming toward the beach.

Since the Japanese had seen the UDT men at Saipan, it was natural to suppose they might now be using swimmers of their own as guards. Perhaps this was one of them. The UDT man drew a knife, his only weapon, and began cautiously to circle.

At this point the other swimmer saw him. Carefully the two men circled, only a few yards apart and getting closer. But just as they reached striking distance they recognized one another. "I thought you were coming *off* the beach," one whispered.

"I wasn't coming anywhere," the other answered. "I was trying to get a bearing from my compass."

Kauffman had an even closer brush with death.

As he swam toward the beach he saw a man he recognized as one of the marines. But the marine got only a brief glimpse of Kauffman and mistook him for a Japanese. Instantly the marine dived. Turning back under water, he came up close behind Kauffman and seized him around the throat, trying to strangle him.

"We had a real rough game of water polo for a few moments," Kauffman said later. "Then I managed to break loose. We came up facing one another and he recognized me."

Kauffman's group was headed toward the southernmost and widest of the two beaches. But when he reached shore and began to crawl cautiously along the beach, he quickly realized that it was not as big as it ought to be. Since Kauffman had flown back and forth over the whole island, studying it from the air, he knew there were only two beaches in the area. Thus he realized that he must be on the northern beach rather than the one to the south. And if the current had carried *him* too far north, then how much farther might it have carried the men who were supposed to explore this beach?

There was nothing he could do about them now, however, and no possibility of reaching the beach to the south. So he began to explore the one he was on. Soon he was joined by the two UDT men who had almost fought one another in the water.

The men had painted their bodies a silver color so they would blend with the white beach, and their heads were covered by gray cowls. They also wore life jackets that could be inflated if necessary, and carried knives in their belts. On hands and knees they searched the entire length and width of the narrow beach, back to where palm trees and underbrush formed a dark wall.

Meanwhile, the men who were supposed to have landed on this beach were having an even more difficult time. They too had lost all contact with one another in the dark and fog.

The commander of the group, Lieutenant John DeBold, found himself swimming alone in the sea. He could hear surf ahead of him, though as yet there was no sign of beach. Suddenly he touched bottom, and at the same moment saw a high cliff looming over him. But there was no beach in sight.

He knew that the current was supposed to be moving south, and that there was a cliff between the two beaches. So he must be opposite that cliff, he thought, and turned northward. The water was only a foot and a half to two feet deep. With only his head above the surface, he lay in the water, pulling himself along with his hands.

In this way he covered a quarter of a mile before

he realized he was going with the current, not against it. He turned and started south again. But with the current against him he made little progress. And by now it was time to rendezvous with the small boat that would carry him back to the ship.

DeBold turned away from the cliff and swam back toward the open sea. The fog was lifting now. Overhead, the moon that had been scurrying in and out of clouds tore free, streaking the tops of the waves with silver. There were no boats in sight.

DeBold had a tiny flashlight in a waterproof container fastened to his belt. He took it out, hoping he could signal one of the boats. But water had managed to seep inside the rubber container, and the flashlight would not work.

All this time the tide was taking him northward. Looking back from the crest of a wave he could see the island vanishing behind him. DeBold inflated his life jacket and began to float, saving his strength. There was no way of knowing what lay ahead.

Suddenly he saw a ship. It was not the small boat he had left hours before, nor was it the *Gilmer*. But it must be American, he thought, since the Japanese were not supposed to have any ships in these waters. Blacked out, a dark shape silhouetted against the moonlit sky, it was passing only a few hundred yards away. If only his flashlight had been working . . .

DeBold snatched off his dive mask. Using it to reflect the moonlight, he began to signal furiously. The ship kept going. Then, at the last moment, it swerved and slowed down.

It was a mine sweeper which had been alerted to the fact that Navy and Marine frogmen were lost in these waters. DeBold was rescued, and soon afterward three marines were found by the same ship.

Off Saipan Admiral Harry Hill had been planning a huge air and sea search for the missing men as soon as daylight arrived. But there was no need for it. The last swimmer was plucked out of the water at four-thirty in the morning.

Even so, the reconnaissance had been a failure. Only one beach had been searched, and it was the less important of the two. So a night later UDT 7 with another group of swimming marines returned to Tinian.

The second reconnaissance went perfectly. The radar on the ship worked flawlessly, and the small boats deposited the swimmers in the water, just where they should have been. All of the men landed on the proper beaches. They found no mines, no fortifications and good exits. The Japanese general on the island had been sure these beaches were too small for a big invasion.

A few days later he was proved wrong. The

marines went ashore, across the beaches and onto the high ground beyond before the Japanese could turn to meet them.

Shortly after Kauffman and his men searched the beaches at Tinian, UDTs 3, 4 and 6 began working at Guam. Guam, a small American Navy base before the war, had been captured by the Japanese just three days after the bombing of Pearl Harbor. The United States Navy was now ready to launch air and surface attacks against the island, even while the fighting continued on Saipan a hundred miles to the north. The Japanese commander knew an invasion was coming, and he had his men working desperately to prepare for it.

At 2:30 P.M. on July 14, 1944, UDT 3 made its first exploration. Small boats carried the men almost to the reef, which was only 200 to 400 yards offshore. Behind them, gunboats loaded with 20- and 40-mm. guns and rows of rockets and machine guns fired steadily over their heads. Beyond the gunboats were the battleship *Idaho*, the cruiser *Honolulu* and two destroyers. The beach was a wall of exploding shells. Since the Japanese commander had decided not to disclose the location of his large guns by firing them, the only return fire came from a few hidden snipers.

A frogman awaits the "go" signal to begin his swim.

From the small boats the UDT men swam in to the reef. At this spot, off what was called Asan Point, the reef was long and flat, completely exposed at low tide and covered only by a foot or two of water at high tide. On top of it the Japanese had built concrete boxes, which were filled with big chunks of coral. The concrete boxes were usually about six feet long, four feet wide, four feet high and only about six feet apart. In between them were tangles of barbed wire. No landing craft could possibly get through to the beach unless these obstacles were destroyed.

After they had mapped this stretch of the reef, the UDT men swam back to their boats. Then they headed south to study the next beach. Here the enemy artillery opened up. Geysers of water shot skyward all around the men and boats. Even so, they were able to finish their preliminary maps.

The American commanders did not want to land on this second beach. But there were two important reasons why it had to be explored, along with all the other beaches. First, it was necessary to know the conditions of the reefs before making a final decision on where to land. And second, when the Japanese saw the Navy frogmen working off all the beaches, they could not be sure where the real attack would fall.

That night Team 3 was back at the reef off Asan Point. In the darkness the men used rubber rafts to paddle from the small boats to the reef. They wore tennis shoes, gloves and kneepads. These guarded against cuts from the sometimes poisonous coral as they mapped the reef and the concrete cribs built on it. Then they moved into the water beyond, heading cautiously toward the beach itself.

All along the beach Japanese soldiers were at work building more coral-filled boxes to prevent enemy tanks from pushing ashore. Cautiously the UDT men slipped closer and closer, with only their faces above the water. In one place the Japanese had set up a concrete mixer, and a UDT man lay in the gently rolling surf and watched. He could hear clearly the conversation of the enemy soldiers. On his plastic tablet he wrote down the location of the new boxes. Then he swam slowly back toward the reef.

At the northern end of the beach Ensign Martin Jacobson finished his reconnaissance and returned to the reef. He crawled across it to where his rubber boat was anchored. One of his men was already there, but the third man who shared the boat had not yet come back. Jacobson waited, and a few minutes later the third frogman came crawling across the reef. Jacobson leaned forward to help him into the rubber boat.

At this moment the moon broke out of the clouds. Immediately a machine gun on the island began to fire. Bullets slashed the water all around the boat; they ricocheted off the reef with wild, whining sounds.

The machine gun stopped. Then it started again. As bullets screamed around him, Jacobson pulled the rubber boat close against the reef for protection.

The moon disappeared under a cloud again. There was a final burst of firing, then silence. "Are you all right?" the Ensign whispered to his men.

"All right," they answered. "You?"

"Yes. Only——" But there was no need to say more. Though none of the men had been touched, their rubber boat had been shot full of holes. It was sinking. The only thing to do now was swim.

They started through the water, hoping to find one of the other rubber boats. But in the darkness they could see no sign of any of them. Then suddenly a flare shot up from their transport. That was the signal for all the boats to return.

For a while the three men swam along the edge of the reef, resting on it now and then. They knew that when they did not return to the APD a search would be made for them. But could they be found in this darkness?

An hour passed. Another. Another. Soon it would be daylight and the Japanese would see them on the reef. Without any protecting fire from the fleet, they would not have a chance. The only thing to do was swim out to sea, out of sight of the Japanese on the island, and hope for the best.

Daylight came slowly. Once a huge fish passed, so close the swimmers could almost have touched it. Perhaps it was a shark. They could not be sure. A moment later, from the direction in which it had disappeared, they heard what might have been more fish, a huge school of them.

Instead it was the destroyer *MacDonough* looming suddenly through the gray mist. The swimmers began to shout at it. A moment later they were sighted, and rescued.

The day scheduled for the actual landing on Guam was known as William Day. (In order to confuse the enemy the word "D Day" was not used for all invasions. The date could be called by any designated letter.) The UDT men had started their work on William minus seven: seven days before the invasion. For four days they worked, sometimes day and night, at exploring and mapping the beaches. Sometimes, in a twenty-four-hour period, they made as many as four trips from the transports to the reefs and beaches.

From some of the reefs long, bony fingers of coral ran out toward the open sea. Sometimes a landing craft taking swimmers to or from the beach would ground on the coral. When this happened the enemy gunners ashore would immediately concentrate their fire on the helpless craft.

One day a landing craft had just picked up John Parrish of Team 3 and was maneuvering to recover a warrant officer named Blowers, when it stuck on a coral head. Blowers continued swimming and reached the boat. But as Parrish leaned over to help him aboard, a single sniper bullet struck the warrant officer in the head, killing him immediately. An instant later, while Parrish was still struggling to pull the body of his friend aboard, Japanese artillery opened fire. As shells burst all around the landing craft, the men aboard worked furiously to free the boat. Another landing craft, moving in to help, also grounded. Then a mortar shell crashed close alongside, wounding several frogmen and members of the boats' crews.

Finally one of the boats got free. All the men piled into it, taking their dead and wounded comrades with them. They left the other craft stuck on the reef.

This was another example of what the demolition teams already knew. While working close to shore in daylight, a man was much safer swimming than he was in a small boat. There were several reasons for this. A lone swimmer offered a very small target. In fact, as long as he could stay under water, he was no target at all. The men had learned that two or three feet below the surface they could catch rifle and machine-gun bullets in their hands without being hurt. Often they brought the bullets back for souvenirs. The UDT men had also learned that the Japanese hesitated to expose the location of their artillery by firing at such an elusive target as a swimmer. On the other hand, any kind of boat offered a clear target, and one that the enemy would usually fire on.

The period of greatest danger occurred whenever a boat working close among the reefs became motionless. Japanese gunners had a difficult time hitting a small boat while it was running a fast zig-zag course. But the moment the boat stopped, they would concentrate all their fire power on it.

This led to the development of a new way of recovering swimmers from the water. Two men would crouch on a rubber raft that was fastened to the offshore side of the landing craft. One of the men would hold a three-foot length of stiff rope with a loop at each end. The landing craft would approach a swimmer at high speed. Raising his arm, the swimmer would hook his elbow in the loop of the rope held toward him by the man on the raft. This would jerk him alongside the rubber raft, and the second man would boost him aboard.

When all the Guam beaches had been explored, the choice of landing areas for the invasion was made. Then, on William minus three, came the order for the demolition teams to start destroying the obstacles off these beaches.

It was at this point, the frogmen said, that their job changed again. "Sneak and peek," had gone out with the daylight swims. Now a better description of their work was, "Wham and scram!" Their small boats were piled high with explosives as they headed toward the reefs. And when the swimmers went into the water they towed rows of twenty-pound packs of tetrytol, each pack fastened to a rubber bladder so it would float. The men tied these explosive packs to the concrete boxes the Japanese had built, and to the barbed wire between them. Then they connected all the packs by detonating cord.

Once this job was completed, all but two of the frogmen would swim back to the boats. These two, the fuse men, stayed behind until they were sure the area had been cleared. Then they cut a fuse long enough to allow them two or three minutes in which to escape before the detonating cord was ignited. Once the cord ignited, it instantly set off all the tetrytol—and a whole section of reef and man-made barriers would go skyward together.

It was a joke among the UDTs that the fuse men were the fastest swimmers in the world. In fact some of them claimed they could swim fifty yards

On William-minus-two-day, an Underwater Demolition unit paddles toward a Guam beach for a coral-blasting expedition.

in the air without ever touching the water.

During nighttime operations around Guam the demolitioneers crossed the reefs to the shallow water beyond, and even to the beaches themselves. One night a UDT officer, quietly tying tetrytol packs to a row of concrete cribs on the beach, heard voices just a little to his right. He thought the noise was coming from some of his own men and angrily walked toward them, meaning to tell them to be quiet. He was close enough to see the men before he realized they were Japanese, working around a concrete mixer.

Either the Japanese did not see him, or thought he was one of them. The UDT officer left a pack of explosives on the beach, connected it with detonating cord, and slipped back to where he had been working. A little later, when this section of the beach was blown up, the Japanese concrete mixer went with it.

On their last trip to the beach, the night before the marines were to invade Guam, four UDT men took along a large piece of plywood. They were heading for what was to be one of the main landing beaches, near the little Guam town of Agat. The UDT men pulled their burden through the shallow water and onto the beach itself. Carefully they propped it up facing the sea. Then they slipped back into the water and swam away.

Next morning when the marines stormed ashore they found waiting for them a sign five feet long by two feet wide. It read:

WELCOME MARINES

AGAT USO TWO BLOCKS

COURTESY UDT 4

"That ought to prove who hits the beach first," a frogman said.

Peleliu and Angaur

With the Marianas—Saipan and Tinian and Guam—safe in American hands, the Underwater Demolition Teams went back to Maui for a short, well-deserved rest. Then once more they began training—perfecting the methods learned under fire and teaching them to the new teams that were being formed.

One of the new teams was UDT 10. Some of the men in Team 10 had originally been in the Office of Strategic Services (OSS). This was a super-secret organization trained to carry out special missions behind enemy lines. As part of their training they had learned the use of swim fins. Transferred to UDT, they brought their fins with them.

At Saipan and Guam some of the Navy frogmen had used fins, or flippers, but others had rejected them. These early fins were of hard rubber. They had to be sandpapered carefully for an exact fit or sores would develop on the men's feet. Also, since the fins were stiff, they were difficult to use and almost impossible to walk in. But the fins of the

A bulldozer tank fires at a Japanese-occupied cave on Peleliu.

OSS-trained men were more pliable. Soon all the teams were practicing with them.

Their days of practice were limited, however, for shortly they were aboard their APDs again, headed for more action.

When General Douglas MacArthur left the remnants of his battered and defeated army in the Philippines in March of 1942, he had announced to the world, "I shall return." Now, a little more than two years later, the United States was closing the jaws of a great nutcracker on the Philippines. From New Guinea, MacArthur and his troops were advancing northward, while the United States Navy was closing in from the east. The Navy's next stop would be the Palau Islands, about halfway between Guam and the Philippines.

There were three important reasons for the capture of these islands. First, the enemy airfields there had to be knocked out of commission, and kept out, if the Navy was to operate in the area with any degree of safety. Second, those same airfields were needed for American planes. And third, because of the vast distances in the Pacific, there was need for an advance refueling base for American ships.

The largest of the Palau group of islands is named Babelthuap, which is spelled in almost as many ways

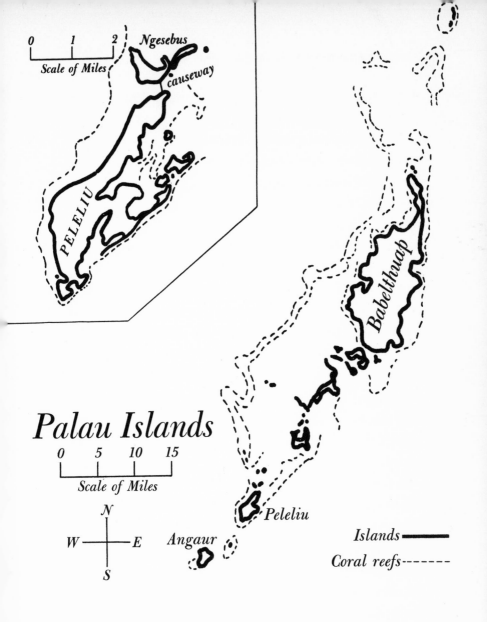

Palau Islands

0   5   10   15
Scale of Miles

N
W —— E
S

Islands ———
Coral reefs ------

Ngesebus
causeway
PELELIU

Babelthuap

Peleliu
Angaur

as it is pronounced. A very mountainous island, it
had been heavily fortified by the enemy. Obviously

its capture would cost the lives of many men.

Back in Hawaii, Admiral Chester Nimitz and his staff decided on a daring plan. If the United States could capture Peleliu and Angaur, two smaller islands near Babelthuap, the Japanese airfields on the big island would be neutralized. Then, with the surrounding waters under control of the United States Navy, the Japanese garrison on Babelthuap, estimated at 25,000 soldiers, could simply be left "to wither on the vine," as Admiral Nimitz put it.

Of the two islands to be invaded, Peleliu was the larger, about five miles long by two miles wide. Angaur, six miles to the southwest, was only about half as big. Both were dotted with beaches and ringed by coral reefs. The water inside the reefs was shallow. Aerial photos off Peleliu, however, had shown dark spots that might be pot holes. Some of these were estimated to be fifty feet deep.

Such holes would cause no trouble if landing craft could cross the reef and take men and tanks directly to the beach. But if the water over the reef was so shallow that landing craft could not cross, then men and tanks would have to be unloaded on the reef. In that case, how would they manage to get over the deep holes in the lagoon?

The job for the UDTs was to discover exactly what the conditions were. Teams 6 and 7 were assigned to investigate the reefs and beaches of Peleliu.

At first things went off as smoothly as could be hoped for. The experience gained in the Marianas and the weeks spent in subsequent training proved their worth. Gunboats and destroyers moved in close to furnish a terrific covering fire. The landing craft carrying the swimmers raced in zigzag lines to dodge enemy guns. Each boat turned parallel to the reef in the proper place. The swimmers went over the side onto the rubber rafts. Hidden from the Japanese by their own landing craft, they then rolled from the rafts into the water in pairs. Keeping under water as much as possible and using their new flippers, they swam to the reefs. Here their mission became more difficult.

The first reconnaissance was in daylight, at low tide. Parts of the reef were completely exposed; other parts were under only a foot or two of water. It was too shallow for swimming. So was much of the water beyond the reefs. The dark spots that appeared on the aerial pictures were caused by grass growing on the bottom, not by deep holes. In such shallow water it was almost impossible for the swimmers to hide from enemy snipers. But because of the heavy covering fire, and because the Japanese did not want to expose the positions of their big guns, all the men carried out the reconnaissance safely. In fact every-thing went almost too smoothly before the invasion.

There was considerable confusion one night, how-ever, when some of the men mistook floating logs for Japanese swimmers because the logs did not answer with the password. Later the men joked that they had seen one another stabbing desperately at the logs with their knives. If so, the logs were the only casualties.

The Japanese had built a forest of obstructions on some of the beaches. But when the swimmers came in to blast them out of the way there was only a minimum of opposition. It was almost as if the enemy was playing possum.

Which was just what he proved to be doing.

The interior of Peleliu is made up of rugged lime-stone ridges, dominated by five peaks. The ridges are pock-marked with caves, and it was to these caves that most of the Japanese had retreated, safe from the bombardments of ships and planes. Many of the caves had connecting tunnels, some with steel doors. Behind these doors artillery could be hidden, then suddenly brought out to blast at the Americans in the valleys below—and hidden again before the American artillery could find them.

When it came time for the actual invasion, marines crossed the UDT-cleared beaches with only

(Left) A lookout directs the covering fire for UDT men setting their charges in the water off Peleliu. *(Right)* More than six thousand pounds of tetrytol explode, marking the successful conclusion of a UDT assignment in the Peleliu campaign.

light opposition. But once ashore they ran into some of the fiercest fighting of the whole Pacific war. Casualties began to mount higher and higher, and more and more troops had to be poured ashore.

Usually, once the invasion forces were ashore, most of the hard work of the Underwater Demolition Teams was complete. But at Peleliu the Japanese kept slipping down from their mountain caves at night to plant new mines in the cleared channels. So each day the swimmers had to make new searches. Also the Japanese kept bringing in reinforcements on barges from the nearby islands. The marines, knowing this, were constantly on guard. Once they opened fire on a platoon of frogmen thinking they were enemy reinforcements. On another occasion the Japanese got unexpected help of a different kind. A school of huge sharks moved into the channel where UDT 10 was working, chasing them out of the water faster than the Japanese had ever been able to do.

Meanwhile, teams 8 and 10 had been busily preparing the way for an invasion of nearby Angaur Island. Here, both the exploratory missions and the actual invasion proceeded smoothly, and the island was secured in four days. But on Peleliu the fighting kept getting worse. It was particularly rough along a high spine of land the marines came to call Bloody Nose Ridge. Nevertheless the Japanese were slowly pushed back toward the northern end of the island.

Just north of Peleliu and separated from it by a strait approximately six hundred yards wide and a mile and a half long is a small island named Ngesebus. Because the Japanese kept sending reinforcements from this island to Peleliu, the Americans decided to make a landing on Ngesebus and clean it out.

At one end of the narrow strait the two islands

were connected by a causeway that would permit an easy crossing on foot. If the Americans tried to use the causeway, however, they would be completely exposed to artillery fire from both Peleliu and Ngesebus. The American command wondered if, instead, men could be sent directly across the strait. The water was shallow—but was it shallow enough for tanks and men to cross under their own power?

To find out, the frogmen made one of the most daring and unusual swims in the history of warfare.

Thirteen men were selected from Teams 6 and 8. Not only would they have to swim the mile and a half length of the strait but, because it was blocked by the causeway at the far end, they would also have to turn around and swim back! This meant a three-mile swim in shallow water under constant enemy fire. And the swimmers on each flank would be within fifty yards of the Japanese-held shores.

UDT men had often swum to within a few yards of an enemy beach. But this time there was a feature that made it far more dangerous than usual. Because the water was so shallow, no ships could be brought in to fire over the swimmers' heads and give them protection.

It was arranged for airplanes to make strafing runs back and forth along both islands while the frogmen swam. But an airplane cannot stand still like a ship and keep pouring in fire. At the very best the thirteen frogmen were going to be unprotected a great deal of the time.

About midafternoon, two small boats brought the swimmers as close to the end of the strait as possible. One by one they went over the side. Keeping fairly well abreast, forming a line all the way across the strait, they began their swim. The water was shallow, in most places only three to four feet deep. The men would swim close against the bottom for as long as possible, then come up for a quick gulp of air, a brief look to determine their location, and a rapid plunge to the bottom again.

American planes roared up and down. They raked the shores and the coral rocks and the palm trees with machine-gun fire. Yet every time the planes passed, Japanese soldiers would pop out of foxholes and from behind trees to start firing at the swimmers. From the high ground inland on both islands mortars rained shells.

Swimming under water the frogmen saw bullets and fragments of shells drift past them in the clear water. "Like confetti at Mardi Gras," one man later said. But there was no time now for collecting souvenirs. Each man thought only of the next time he must surface for breath. He knew the next mortar shell might strike so close that the concussion would crush him internally.

Yet not a frogman turned back. A mile and a half they went, through water that was never more than four feet deep. Finally they reached the causeway at the far end of the strait.

On the return trip, all the men swam closer to the middle to verify the depths there. This took them a little farther from the snipers and machine guns, but it also tended to bunch them more closely under the mortars.

They were a lucky thirteen. In the gathering dusk, after three hours in the water under constant enemy fire, they regained their boats. Incredible as it seems, not a man had been wounded.

Meanwhile UDT 10, which had completed its work on Angaur, was sent to the island of Ulithi to the northeast. If the island could be captured, its tremendous lagoon would form a superb harbor for the fleet.

At Ulithi, the water was deep enough for the fleet to come close in shore. They put down a tremendous bombardment, while the UDT men explored the beaches and then blew channels through the reef.

The invasion itself was strangely quiet and peaceful, for the enemy had already abandoned Ulithi. There wasn't a Japanese soldier left on the island.

Frogmen Meet Kamikazes in the Philippines

By the fall of 1944 the time had come for the United States to fulfill General MacArthur's promise to return to the Philippines. In New Guinea, and at Manus in the Admiralty Islands, two vast fleets began to assemble for the invasion. The Underwater Demolition Teams went to Manus.

Here the men had a short period of rest. And here some of them, like John Parrish of UDT 3, first discovered how much fun there could be in underwater swimming when it was done under peaceful conditions.

The Admiralty Islands are just south of the Equator, but the weather is tempered by the balmy water around them. Parrish found them beautiful. A lean youngster with a quick smile and short-cropped dark hair, he had been born in Alabama. After he joined the United States Navy, he spent many months aboard crowded ships going back and forth across the Pacific.

When the Navy asked for volunteers for the new

The USS Ommaney Bay *aflame after an attack by a Japanese suicide plane.*

Underwater Demolition Teams, Parrish joined. "I didn't have any idea what underwater demolition was," he said later. "I knew it was extra hazardous duty, because I was told that when I volunteered. But I had heard the teams trained in Florida. And I was willing to take any kind of duty, if I could get a trip home first."

It was true that most UDTs were training in Florida. But Parrish did not get his trip home. Instead he was sent to the Hawaiian Islands for training, and from there to the invasion of Guam.

At Manus, Parrish had his first opportunity for rest and recreation in many months. With some of the other frogmen he spent hours swimming in the crystal-clear water, looking at the fantastically colored reefs and the tropical fish as brilliant as butterflies. Sometimes he went swimming with the natives, who wore goggles made of bamboo with paper-thin sea shells for glass.

"I thought I had seen all the reefs I would ever want to see at Guam," Parrish told a friend several years later. "But it was different with nobody shooting at you. I had a wonderful time at Manus. I think it was there I decided I would stay in the Navy, and in UDT, even after the war was over."

But at this time the war was far from over. Parrish and his friends had only a few weeks of leisure before they were back on their APDs. This time they were headed for the island of Leyte in the Philippines, to take part in the greatest invasion of the Pacific war up to that point.

Before the men ever arrived at their destination, however, a tremendous typhoon came roaring across the Pacific. The fleet tried to dodge it, but on October 16 the ships ran head on into winds of more than a hundred miles an hour. Gigantic waves tossed the little APDs about, like feathers blown by an electric fan. Men who had been sailors for years were seasick.

By October 17 the worst of the storm had passed. The scattered ships began to reassemble and move on toward Leyte. A Day, as the invasion date was called, was set for October 20, 1944. But the Underwater Demolition Teams were to begin their work on A minus two, October 18.

The typhoon had buffeted the little mine sweepers that preceded the fleet even harder than it had hit the APDs. Consequently by the afternoon of the eighteenth, they had not been able to complete their job of clearing away the mines in the deep water off the landing beaches. As a result the battleships and cruisers, which were to provide covering fire for the swimmers, had to stay far offshore, using only their big guns. Even the destroyers had to stay two miles or more away from the beaches.

To make matters worse, the operational plan for the invasion incorrectly stated that the Underwater Demolition Teams did *not* want air support. Actually, they needed it desperately. So when the frogmen's landing craft headed for the beaches, they had very little covering fire and no air support.

On the shore ahead of them waited some of Japan's most highly trained soldiers. When the small boats of the UDT men were within a half-mile of the beach, the Japanese opened up with everything they had.

John Parrish and the other swimmers from UDT 3 got into the water without being hit. The sea was still rough from the storm and so muddy that there was almost no visibility. This made it difficult for the frogmen to take soundings and search for mines and other obstacles, but it also interfered with Japanese attempts to bring accurate fire to bear on the swimmers. The men of UDT 3 were able to complete their reconnaissance without mishap.

Teams 4, 5 and 8 were not so lucky. The boat carrying Platoon 2 of Team 4 launched its swimmers. But before it could turn away it was hit by two mortar shells. Three men were wounded; the rest were knocked down by the concussion. The boat lay awash in the waves, sinking. The radioman

UDT men speed back to their ship after completing a mission off the shores of Leyte.

called frantically for help, but there was no time. A third and fourth shell hit the boat.

As it went down the uninjured men inflated the life jackets of the wounded and got them into the water. Swimming, they towed them away from the shore with shells still bursting around them.

The team's APD, the *Goldsborough,* seeing what was happening, moved closer to give all possible fire support. Then it too was hit by a Japanese shell that killed two men and wounded sixteen. Even so, the APD continued to pour fire against the enemy hidden ashore.

Team 5 was the only group to have air support that day. While the planes strafed the beach, the frogmen battled the rolling surf and murky water to search for mines. Sure at last that there were none, they headed back to their landing craft. As the boats came in to pick up the swimmers, the Japanese fire concentrated on them. On one of the boats a machine gunner was killed by sniper fire. A mortar burst wounded another.

At the same time Team 8 was having its troubles. Ensign Donald Nourse had just gone into the water and was swimming toward the beach when mortar shells struck close to him. He dived, and at that same moment another shell exploded, only a few yards away. The concussion smashed his diving mask into his face, cutting it and injuring his eyes. Almost blinded he turned back and swam toward the boat that had dropped him. But he could not see well enough to hook his arm through the pickup ring. The landing craft had to stop dead in the water to lift him aboard.

Edward Tilton, another frogman, knelt beside Nourse to give first aid. And in that moment, before the boat could get under way, a sniper's bullet struck Tilton in the back and killed him.

A little later a mortar shell struck another of Team 8's landing craft while it was picking up swimmers.

Four were wounded.

It was the bloodiest day yet for frogmen in the Pacific. But of all those killed and wounded only one man, Ensign Nourse, had been hit while in the water.

Team 9 had a similar tragic experience the next day, while working on beaches just north of those explored the day before. The boat carrying Platoon 4 launched its swimmers, but the landing craft carrying Platoon 1 was hit and sunk before the frogmen could get into the water. One man was killed, and twelve were wounded. Platoons 2 and 3 rescued the wounded and took them back to the ship. Then they returned and finished their work, this time without any casualties.

Shortly after Leyte came the invasion of Luzon, the chief island of the Philippines. And here the frogmen first met the full force of a new and terrible weapon: the Kamikazes, the suicide planes of the Japanese.

The UDTs were scheduled to make their first swim off Luzon on January 7, 1945. The afternoon of January 4 they were on their APDs, off the central Philippines, heading north. Surrounding them were carriers, battleships, cruisers and destroyers—the great battle fleet that would lay down the pre-invasion bombardment.

Suddenly there was the sound of gunfire. And all at once a terrible burst of flame from the light carrier *Ommaney Bay* lit up the darkening water. A single Japanese plane—somehow undetected by radar, unseen until it was within a few hundred yards of the carrier—had crashed head on into the ship. This suicide attack set both the carrier and the planes on its decks afire. Tanks of aviation gasoline began to explode. Within a few minutes the *Ommaney Bay* was one great burning mass and had to be abandoned. Later it was sunk by an American destroyer.

Only one other Kamikaze came that afternoon, and it missed the carrier it tried to hit. But the next day brought an experience that would never be forgotten by any man in the fleet who lived through it.

All morning the Japanese planes attacked. All morning they were knocked down by the defending American planes before they could reach the ships. But in the late afternoon came an attack that could not be turned back. Some of the planes flew so high they could barely be seen, glittering in the late afternoon sunlight. Others skimmed just over the water. Some were shot down by the American planes. But others broke through, hurtling headlong at the great procession of ships.

The American fleet was accustomed to conventional air attacks, but this was different. These pilots were not trying to drop their bombs or torpedoes and return to base. Like the pilots of the night before they came with but one purpose: to die. Their method of dying was to crash their planes and themselves against the United States ships.

Because the Underwater Demolition Teams were not part of the ships' crews, most of them had no battle stations. On a few transports they manned machine guns. But most of them could only stand and watch.

As the planes bored in, the guns of the fleet put up an almost solid wall of fire. One plane after another disintegrated, yet some managed to break through. One of them, on fire, with parts tearing loose, plunged head on into the cruiser *Louisville*. Another hit the *Australia*. Another smashed so close alongside the *Arunta* that her engines were knocked out of commission.

The American fleet continued to hold its course. And the Japanese suicide planes kept coming. The destroyer escort *Stafford* was hit, and had to be taken in tow. Then two planes hit the light carrier *Manila Bay*. Her skipper, Captain Fitzhugh Lee, told about it later:

"Both Jap planes were beautifully handled. They came in low at high speed, weaving slightly, and strafing during the approach. When about 1,000 yards from the ship, they pulled into sharp, climbing turns, turned over almost on their backs, then straightened out and dove straight into the ship from an altitude of about 800 feet."

But the fires started aboard the *Manila Bay* were extinguished. The ship stayed afloat. The fleet kept going. So far none of the ships carrying UDTs had been hit, but the frogmen stared in awe at the terrifying death dives of the planes above them.

Aboard the *Badger* the men of UDT 8 saw three

The USS Manila Bay *is shown a few seconds after a Kamikaze crashed onto her decks.*

Kamikazes diving at the ship at one time. The suicide planes flashed down through the cloud of anti-aircraft fire, flaming, falling apart, coming closer —and then missing, plunging into the sea close by.

The men of UDT 10, on the *Rathburne,* saw a Kamikaze plunge straight for them. When it seemed certain the plane would crash into the ship exactly where the men stood, a half dozen of them dived over the side. But the plane missed the ship by inches, sweeping just over it and into the sea on the far side. When the swimmers were picked up, one of them said jokingly, "We weren't deserting our battle stations, because we don't have any. Besides, our job is in the water."

The next day, January 6, 1945, the American fleet entered Lingayen Gulf. Here it was necessary to clear away any mines that might be found, and to bombard the shore defenses before the frogmen made their swim. Once again the Kamikazes came swarming in like a horde of gigantic and insane bees. The attack was even worse than on the previous afternoon.

Two destroyers were hit at almost the same instant. A few minutes later a Kamikaze crashed into the battleship *New Mexico.* Another plunged into a third destroyer, and another hit a mine sweeper. But the rest of the mine sweepers kept working, and the shore bombardment continued.

Then swiftly a new wave of Kamikazes swept in to the attack. The cruiser *Columbia* was hit once, then again. A suicide plane crashed into the battleship *California*. Within the next fourteen minutes, five more ships were hit.

Yet still the fleet kept firing, pounding the beach, knocking down enemy planes. On the *Badger*, UDT men counted thirty-five Japanese planes crashing into the water within a single half-hour. In their excitement they may sometimes have counted the same plane twice. But wherever they looked, the sky was filled with bursting shells and planes.

By comparison the swim to the Luzon beaches next day was almost peaceful. As at Leyte, there was heavy surf. Visibility in the murky water was poor, and the frogmen had to search more by feel than by sight. They found no mines and no prepared obstacles on the beach. This too had been true at Leyte. Possibly there were so many beaches in the Philippines that the Japanese had despaired of blocking them all and so relied on counterattacks by guns and troops ashore.

At Luzon the ships carrying the UDTs did not leave the scene once the beaches had been explored and cleared. Instead they stayed to help fight the Kamikazes. Now, in addition to planes, the Japanese were using small suicide boats with torpedoes fastened to them. And for the first time Japanese swimmers began to appear, trying to push mines against the sides of American ships.

On the *Belknap* the frogmen of UDT 9 saw two Japanese swimmers a mile offshore. They had no mine with them. Perhaps they had lost it; perhaps they had been in one of the small boats that had been sunk. They were swimming toward Luzon. The *Belknap* put over a boat with several frogmen in it, meaning to take the Japanese prisoners. But as the boat came close, the swimmers suddenly produced hand grenades. A machine gunner in the bow killed them before they could throw the grenades into the boat.

Before that day was over, the frogmen killed nine other Japanese swimmers who refused to surrender.

Meanwhile the Kamikaze planes were still coming. And on the next day, January 12, one of them struck the *Belknap*. Eleven frogmen were killed and thirteen wounded.

But not even Kamikazes could turn back the great American fleet or the troops it put ashore. More and more soldiers were poured into the islands; more and more supplies were piled on the beaches. There were long days of fighting still ahead, but eventually the Philippines would be recaptured.

Iwo Jima

Iwo Jima is a tiny island, less than five miles long and about two miles wide. The earth is fairly rich but rugged, with a dormant volcano named Mount Suribachi rising conelike from the southern tip of the island. Before the war a handful of natives, under the control of the Japanese government, lived on Iwo Jima.

Since the island had no harbor, few ships ever stopped there. And the Japanese made no effort to improve the place. There was little to improve, nothing of value. Around the world probably not one person in thirty thousand had ever heard of Iwo Jima.

Yet it was to become one of the bloodiest battlefields in all history, and for just one reason. It lay halfway between Tokyo and the American airfields in the Mariana Islands—approximately 700 miles from each.

American B-29s flying out of the Marianas to bomb Japan were faced with a 3,000-mile round trip.

American beach crews attempt to free boats grounded on the shores of Iwo Jima.

Because of the distance, they could carry only a minimum weight of bombs, and fighter planes could not accompany them. But while the enemy held Iwo Jima, Japanese fighters could rise off its two airfields to intercept the American Superfortresses, both going and returning. Also, radar stations on Iwo could flash an early warning to the homeland.

The United States needed Iwo. After the war an official publication of the United States Army Air Force would write:

> To every B-29 crew who flew to Japan after March, 1945, (after Iwo had been captured) the fact that Iwo had become a U.S. base was a cause for thanksgiving. . . . If you had engine trouble, you held out for Iwo. If the weather was too rough, you held out for Iwo. Formations assembled over Iwo, and gassed up at Iwo for extra long missions. If you needed fighter escort, it usually came from Iwo. If you had to ditch or bail out, you knew that air-sea rescue units were sent from Iwo. Even if you never used Iwo as an emergency base, it was a psychological benefit. It was there to fall back on.

Ever since the invasion of Tarawa, the Navy had been training new Underwater Demolition Teams. When the order came to take Iwo Jima, Teams 12, 13, 14 and 15 were assigned to take part in the

On the decks of an APD, Underwater Demolition men prepare for a mission.

invasion. Team 15 was destined to suffer the heaviest loss of any UDT in the Pacific war.

On the morning of February 16, 1945, the APDs with the accompanying fleet came in sight of the little island with its volcano rising steeply out of the sea. It was a rainy day. Squalls came and went across the sea. The APDs moved to within a mile and a quarter of the island and circled it. The frogmen crowded along the rails, trying to learn all they could before their scheduled swim the next day.

111

Iwo had once looked green against the blue ocean, but for months planes had been bombing it. And the fleet had shelled it time and again. What the frogmen could see through the rain squalls looked like a desert, without signs of life.

There were two long beaches, and the sand was a volcanic black color rather than white. One beach was on the eastern side, one on the western. The officers commanding the invasion preferred to land on the eastern beach, if possible, because it was somewhat more protected from waves. But the approaches to both would have to be searched. The frogmen were to reconnoiter the eastern beach on the morning of the seventeenth. They would scout the western beach in the afternoon.

The seventeenth was clear and sunny; the ocean, beautifully blue. Several miles offshore the battleships and cruisers took up their positions and began a slow, steady firing. From what looked like a deserted island there was no answer.

Quickly the destroyers and destroyer escorts darted between the heavier vessels and raced to within a mile of the beach. Here they turned parallel to the island and began to fire, while the big ships continued to pour in shells over their heads. The APDs followed the destroyers, lining up close behind them. Small boats, already loaded with their crews and carrying ten frogmen in each boat, swung from the davits of the APDs. Without the mother ship's ever stopping, the small boats were lowered into the water. But for a few minutes they were held close alongside, still sheltered by the APDs and the destroyers.

Then came the LCI(G)s—landing craft, infantry, converted to gunboats. Loaded with machine guns, rockets, 20- and 40-millimeter guns, they passed between the destroyers and moved to within a half-mile of the beach. They were to provide the point-blank fire cover needed by the swimmers. As the gunboats moved forward, the small boats carrying the frogmen darted out from the APDs. They raced past the destroyers, past the gunboats, flashing in zigzag lines to within a quarter-mile of the beach to drop their swimmers.

Perhaps, as at Leyte, the Japanese mistook this for the actual invasion. Abruptly from all over the island —from the sides of Mount Suribachi to the left of the beach, from the high cliffs to the right, from the plateau land between—a terrible fire poured down.

This time the fire centered on the gunboats rather than the small craft carrying the swimmers. The gunboat from which Commander Kauffman was directing the UDTs took a direct hit from an eight-inch shell. The radioman standing beside Kauffman was killed, though the Commander was not touched. Then another shell, another and another smashed into the boat. Quickly its guns were knocked out and it began to list.

Kauffman ordered the boat out of the line. Another one that had been held in reserve took its place, and Kauffman transferred to it. Almost immediately it too was hit, time and again. Soon it was a mass of fire and had to be ordered to retire. By now every one of the twelve gunboats had been hit. One was sunk, and ten others were put out of commission. Kauffman transferred to a destroyer.

As he was climbing aboard, the skipper, an old friend of Kauffman's, leaned over the side and shouted, "You Jonah! Why do you have to pick my ship?"

The swimmers, meanwhile, were heading toward the beach through the cold water and hot gunfire. Iwo was far north of any previously invaded island. As protection against the cold water, all the swimmers had been coated with cocoa butter. Despite this, some of them got cramps. A few had to turn back to the boats, although they knew by now that the boats were especially dangerous. The other frogmen kept going.

In the clear water they could make their soundings without difficulty. They could also see the bullets and shrapnel drifting around them when they were swimming under water. "As thick as snowflakes," one man said later.

Back on the destroyers the commanding officer ordered a barrage of phosphorus shells. This threw up a screen of white smoke between the swimmers and the Japanese gunners. But it was a thin screen that swirled in the wind. Frequently a frogman, looking up, could see the muzzles of machine guns and rifles poking through the slits of camouflaged pillboxes. They seemed to be aimed straight at him as they fired.

Even so, most of the men reached the beach. They swam along it, collecting the black sand in tobacco cans which they carried in their belts. The sand would be analyzed by experts on the ships. In this way more could be learned about the condition of the beach itself. Only when their work was done did the frogmen head back to sea.

Off Red Beach two men of Team 12 had located some submerged rocks. They tied buoys to them so the invasion landing craft would not go aground. When the job was finished, they started to swim away, but one of the men was washed back onto the rocks by the tide. The boat that was .to pick him up could not come close without being grounded. In an effort to reach the boat, the frogman once more tried to swim away. Once more the sucking water around the rocks pulled him back.

By now the Japanese had seen what was happening, and they started firing shells all around the area. The boat dodged frantically, waiting for the struggling man to swim free. For a few moments he clung to the rocks, resting. Then, taking advantage of a wave as it swirled out away from the rocks, he plunged in and fought his way free.

But now he was too tired to catch the noose that was tossed to him from the dodging pickup boat. Twice it missed him. Twice he went under as the boat passed. Finally the boat came in a third time and stopped dead in the water while the swimmer was lifted aboard. Then it got out of there, fast.

By this time all the gunboats, badly hit, had been forced out of line. All the small boats had rescued their swimmers and retired—all, that is, except one. This also was a boat from Team 12, searching for a frogman named A. E. Anderson. He could not be found. The boat came within a hundred yards of the beach, so close it was in danger of being caught in the surf and swept ashore. Japanese fire poured around it. Finally, ten minutes after the deadline for the return of all the boats, it was ordered back to the fleet. Although there had been other casualties aboard the landing craft and gunboats, Anderson was the only swimmer lost in all that shell-torn water.

The afternoon swim, compáred to the one in the morning, turned out to be quite painless. During the morning a number of heavy Japanese guns, carefully camouflaged, had revealed their positions by firing on the gunboats. Consequently they had been knocked out by the big guns of the fleet. Also, by afternoon, the Japanese understood this was not yet the actual invasion. The swimmers met only machine-gun and sniper fire. All returned safely from their assignments.

Only a few mines were discovered off Iwo Jima, and these the UDTs destroyed without difficulty. There was no coral reef. Close to the shore the water was deep enough for landing craft to come in. Two days after the frogmen made their search, the marines came ashore with only a minimum of casualties. They advanced inland with little opposition, and supplies began to pour in behind them.

Then, just as on Peleliu, the situation changed. The Japanese had deliberately held their fire. Their plan was to wait until a number of marines had landed, then smash the supplies and craft behind them on the beaches. In this way the Japanese would cut them off and destroy them.

Their strategy almost worked. Within a few

As they approach the southern tip of Iwo Jima, invading marines sight Mount Suribachi.

minutes after the hidden Japanese guns opened fire, the beach was littered with wrecked landing craft. Supplies and ammunition were in flames. Marines charging inland had passed Japanese pillboxes hidden in the sand. In some places these hidden concrete boxes, manned by machine-gun crews, were only a few feet apart. There were hundreds upon hundreds of them. And as on Peleliu the whole island was a honeycomb of fortified caves and tunnels. All at once the marines found themselves being fired on from every side.

Also, someone had made a mistake in analyzing the black sand brought back by the frogmen. Along the beach it had been packed hard by the waves. But a few feet beyond the water the sand was powder fine. The jeeps and armored cars sank into it and stalled. Only vehicles with caterpillar treads could move.

Soon the beach was so littered with wrecked craft there was no room for the new ones bringing troops and supplies. So the UDTs had a new job: blasting away their own wrecked craft instead of coral reefs. While they worked, the Japanese rained fire down upon them.

But even so the frogmen again suffered their heaviest losses while on shipboard. On the night before the invasion the *Blessman,* with UDT 15 on board, was in the picket line of ships surrounding the island. It was dark and quiet. Only a few enemy planes had attacked the fleet. There had been no huge Kamikaze raids such as those at Luzon. On board the *Blessman* the frogmen were writing letters home or playing cards.

Then it happened, totally without warning. A Japanese plane swooped out of the night, dropped two bombs, and was gone. One bomb exploded close alongside the *Blessman.* The other crashed through the deck into the messroom where the men were sitting, and exploded.

Almost instantly the ship was afire. Wounded men tried to help others more seriously wounded. Some reached the forward part of the ship, some the stern. Amidships there was only a mass of flame. Every man aboard knew that the ship carried tons and tons of tetrytol. Once the fire reached the tetrytol, the *Blessman* would explode like one huge bomb.

Most of the ship's pumps had been knocked out, so the men formed bucket lines to fight the fire. The majority of the surviving frogmen were on the stern. As they passed buckets, even helmets, full of sea water dipped from over the side of the ship, they sang "Anchors Aweigh." All the time they wondered about the tetrytol, but they kept singing, and fighting the flames.

Commander Kauffman was on the *Gilmer,* the closest ship to the *Blessman* when she was hit. He led a boarding party to help fight the fire. Then the *Gilmer* came alongside, so close the ships almost touched. If the *Blessman* exploded, the *Gilmer* would go with her. But water from the *Gilmer's* hoses could be poured onto the flames.

Eventually the fire was put out. Emergency repairs were made, and the wounded were transferred to another ship. The dead were buried at sea, just off the little island whose name few had known a year before.

UDT 15 had lost eighteen men killed and twenty-three wounded. This was over forty percent of the team, the heaviest loss ever suffered by an Underwater Demolition Team in the Pacific.

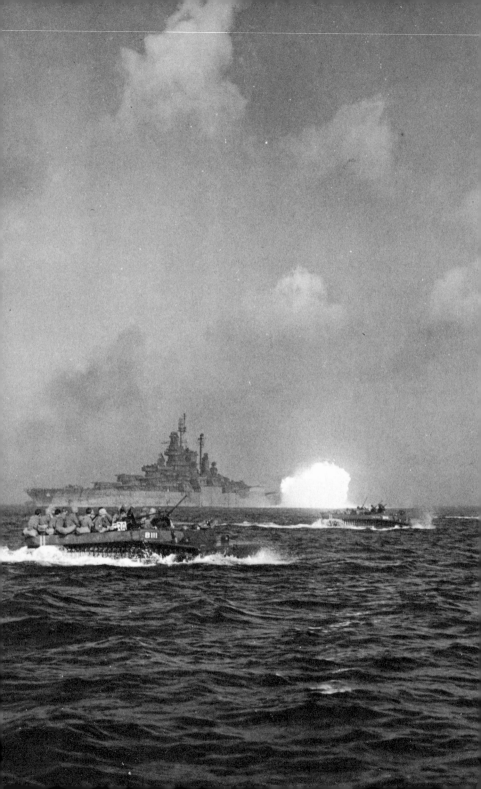

Okinawa and
a Thousand Frogmen

With Iwo Jima in American hands there was one more step to be taken before the United States would be ready for the invasion of Japan itself. The Army needed a big island, closer to Japan than the Marianas, to use as a base from which great fleets of bombers could fly out carrying heavy loads. And the Navy needed a supply base.

The one island that filled both needs was Okinawa. It was only 325 miles from the southern tip of Japan, only 900 miles from Tokyo. The terrain was rugged, but the island stretched out to a length of seventy miles and many airfields could be built on it. And with its surrounding clusters of small islands, it offered excellent harbors.

So Okinawa was the next inevitable step in the march toward Japan. The Japanese, of course, were aware of this. They put 100,000 troops on the island, and fortified it until it bulged with guns and men.

Against Okinawa the United States sent the greatest force of men and ships ever assembled in the

A U.S. battleship provides protective fire as amtracks head for Okinawa.

Pacific war. There were whole fleets of carriers. There were new, fast battleships armed with sixteen-inch cannon that could shoot a distance of more than twenty miles. Some of these ships carried as many as 150 anti-aircraft guns. There were cruisers, destroyers, transports—everything down to PT boats and the rubber rafts of the frogmen. And for this invasion there were to be ten Underwater Demolition Teams of approximately one hundred men each—a thousand frogmen.

The UDTs had come a long way since that day at Kwajalein when Lew Luehrs and Bill Acheson stripped off their uniforms to dive over the side of their landing craft.

The invasion date was Easter Sunday, April 1, 1945. The code name for the day was L or Love Day. The troops said it was April Fool's Day for the Japanese. Whatever its name, the frogmen's work started well ahead.

About fifteen miles west of Okinawa is a group of small islands called the Kerama Retto. The American commanders decided to capture these first so they could be used as a seaplane base and a harbor during the attack on the main island.

On the morning of March 25 (Love minus seven, as the military dispatches would refer to it) Teams 12, 13 and 19 made the first swim. There were

Okinawa
and Neighboring Islands

0   5   10   15   20

Scale of Miles

N

W —|— E

S

Ie Shima

Okinawa

EAST CHINA SEA

Keise Shima

Kerama Retto

PACIFIC OCEAN

islands all around them as they started toward their assigned beaches. But overhead thundered a tremendous covering fire from battleships, gunboats and everything in between. A cloud of planes strafed the land ahead of them.

The Japanese commander had crowded practically all his troops on the big island of Okinawa, so resistance in the Kerama Retto was slight. Some of the frogmen said they suffered worse from the cold than from the Japanese. Although Okinawa is about on a parallel with Florida, the weather in April is cold, and the water is colder. The swimmers coated their bodies with aluminum-colored axle grease. This was both for camouflage and for protection against the weather. But it seemed to protect them better from the Japanese snipers than from the cold.

In fact one platoon from Team 19 must have decided the water was just too cold for swimming. The men were approaching a very small islet that appeared to be deserted. Although they had no covering fire from the fleet, they decided that instead of swimming they would paddle their rubber boat right to the beach. Not a shot was fired at them. Even when they reached the beach itself there was no sign of the enemy.

Ensign Bill Cullen, in command of the platoon, wore a pistol; the rest of the men were armed only with knives. But since there seemed to be no enemy on the islet, the men left their boat and started to explore.

At this point Japanese soldiers, hidden back of a cluster of rocks, opened fire. Cullen was wounded twice, once through the leg and once through the wrist of the hand in which he was holding his pistol. As Cullen dropped his gun, Ensign Bob Killough grabbed it and began to fire. Crouching back of a rock, he held off the Japanese while the other men carried Cullen back to the rubber boat and got away. Then, his ammunition gone, Killough followed as fast as he could. Later he claimed he swam the first hundred yards from the beach without touching the water with anything except his fingertips.

There were few man-made obstacles on the Kerama Retto beaches, but the frogmen learned that the water off some beaches was too shallow for the landing craft which were to be used. This information was rushed to the commanders on the transports, and the invasion plans were changed. As a result, American lives were saved.

Indeed, more lives were saved by the early capture of Kerama Retto than anyone had expected. The Japanese had prepared hundreds of small suicide boats like those used at Luzon, and most of them were hidden in the Kerama Retto islands. On the day before the American fleet's arrival, many of the Japanese boat pilots had gone over to Okinawa for a briefing. When Kerama Retto was occupied by the Americans, the pilots could not get back to their craft.

Even so, there were still many suicide boats in Japanese hands. These would slip out at night, and their pilots would try to ram them and their torpedoes against the sides of the American ships. As a defense, the ships put out what they called "Fly Swatter Patrols," small boats armed with 20- and 40-millimeter guns to circle around the big ships and protect them.

Soon the Kamikaze planes began to attack. At first they did not appear in as great numbers as at Luzon. There were just enough to keep the men alert, never knowing at what instant the suicide planes might attack.

American soldiers discovered this camouflaged Japanese suicide boat on an island near Okinawa.

Some of the new UDTs at Okinawa had been in training for more than a year before they arrived there for their first taste of combat. One of these was Team 11, and one of its members was a wide-grinning, curly-haired young man named Ed Higgins. Later Higgins wrote an engrossing book about his experiences, called *Webfooted Warriors*. In it he told of his first combat swim on March 29, off the western shore of Okinawa.

Behind him, as he and his comrades headed toward the low reef, there were 1,000 guns of the fleet for every swimmer. The sound of their firing was overwhelming, deafening. Ahead of the swimmers the whole island seemed to be exploding. Even so, Higgins kept hearing what seemed to be a machine gun following close behind him. He had been in the water several minutes, he said, before he realized it was the sound of his own teeth chattering.

He reached the reef and found that the Japanese had erected hundreds and hundreds of heavy posts, in rows three deep. Higgins noted this on the plastic tablet that hung around his neck. Then, with his swim buddy, Ensign Park, he dived to check the depth and shape of the reef.

After they had been working for several minutes, he noticed that each time he came up for air the water close around him would suddenly shoot up in small geysers. For a moment he did not understand why. Then he realized he and Park were being fired at from the shore.

They began to work faster and faster, not only because of the Japanese fire, but also because of the cold water. The longer they were in the water, the colder it got. Cramps began to knot the muscles in Higgins' legs and he had trouble straightening them. Finally his work was finished. But now he and Park had to wait for the small boat to come and pick them up.

A swimmer in distress could raise both arms over his head as a signal for the rescue boat to come directly to him. But Higgins knew that every man in the team must be as cold and exhausted as he was. He fought to stay afloat, and waited his turn. Since he was at the end of the line, all the others had to be picked up first. Finally the landing craft raced down to him, the rubber pickup boat tied alongside. He raised his arm, hooked it in the pickup noose, and was jerked aboard. There he was bundled in blankets and fed hot coffee.

Back on the transport all his information had to be given to the intelligence officers even before there was time for a hot bath and food. Then almost immediately the planning for the next day's work began. All the thousands of posts Higgins and his

Lieutenant Edward Higgins

comrades had found wedged in the coral reef would
have to be destroyed.

Next came the long job of preparing the demolition
packs. This time they were made of two-and-a-half-
pound blocks of tetrytol. Around each block of
explosive the men wrapped a piece of detonating
cord, which they tied with a special knot. Enough
cord was left dangling to enable the men to fasten
it to the main trunk line that would connect all the
packs. Thus they could all be ignited together. Then

each block of tetrytol was put into a "Schantz pack," a kind of apron with four pockets. When these were filled a float was attached to the Schantz pack so it could be towed by a swimmer.

It took until three in the morning to get the demolition packs ready. Then the men were able to get only two hours' sleep before general quarters sounded. The Kamikazes were coming again. But even with the fleet under attack the frogmen had work of their own. There was more briefing, because every man, every platoon, every team had to know exactly what its task was.

The last thing Higgins did before climbing into the landing craft was to put on the top half of his winter underwear. It would be heavy when wet, but he hoped it would help protect him against the cold. "What it really did," he said later, "was make things a lot hotter than I wanted them."

He was scarcely in the water, swimming toward the reef, before he realized that enemy fire was lashing the water around him more than around either of the men next to him. But why? he wondered, diving, staying under water as long as he could, coming up for a fast breath and diving again. Why should the Japanese concentrate on him?

The swimmers reached the reef and went to work. Around Higgins the enemy fire stayed hot. When

UDT men aboard an APD prepare tetrytol blocks for a blasting
job.

he started swimming toward his friend Norm Elliott, Elliott swam in the opposite direction, fast. "Get away from me!" he yelled over his shoulder. "You and that crazy white shirt!"

So that was it! Higgins thought.

The white shirt was making him a fine target for the Japanese snipers. But now, with a knife tied to his wrist and with his load of explosives, he had no chance to get it off. All he could do was keep on with his work and remember the training he had been given back in Florida. He swam under water from one post to the next, coming up for a breath only when the post was between him and the enemy. Then he tied on the pack, fastened it to the trunk line, and swam under water to the next post.

Eventually the job was done. All the men except the fuse pullers swam away from the reef and were picked up by their boats. The fuse pullers cut their fuses and came flying through the water like Olympic racers. Then they too were picked up. The boats went racing away from the island with all the frogmen looking back and waiting.

With a tremendous roar all the reef exploded—all except one part to the left of where Higgins and Team 11 had been working. Here something had gone wrong with the work of Team 16. Most of their obstacles were left undamaged in the water. All the men of Team 11 felt sorry for Team 16, which would have to go back again to finish its job.

`Their sympathy was short-lived. They had been back on their transport only a short time when they learned that Team 11 had been selected to go back and finish the job for Team 16.

Now followed another afternoon and night of long briefings, more hours of work preparing demolition charges, and more briefings. For the third night in a row the men got little if any sleep. Each one realized that every time frogmen went into an area the Japanese learned more and more about how they worked, and how to bring fire to bear on them. On the following day, Team 11 would be making its third trip in three days to the same place. Not even the Japanese, the men thought, were going to keep missing forever.

As Ed Higgins climbed into his platoon boat the next morning he felt sharp pains in his stomach. But he decided they were the result of nervous tension, lack of sleep, and all the coffee he had drunk trying to stay awake. Probably all the other men were feeling them too.

So he said nothing. He went into the water alongside his swim buddy—without the white shirt this time—and headed for the reef. Behind the swimmers the guns of the fleet roared faster than ever. But from caves that pock-marked the inland hills, mortars and machine guns fired back with more concentration than on the previous day.

For Ed Higgins, however, the pain in his stomach was now worse than the fear of enemy shells. But he thought it might be fear that was causing the pain. And perhaps it was the salt water he had swallowed that was making him vomit. And it could be the cold that was causing the cramps in his stomach and legs.

He kept swimming, and continued to tie on the tetrytol packs. When the job was finally finished, he started away from the reef. But now he could hardly swim. The vomiting got worse. He was barely able to catch the rescue loop and be flipped onto the rubber raft, barely able to climb from that into the boat. When he was offered hot coffee, he could not swallow it. Offered a drink of brandy he became violently ill.

"That's when I knew I was really bad off," he said later. "I just lay there and figured that . . . I must be about to die."

In the transport's sickbay a doctor bent over him and gently poked his drawn stomach muscles with a finger. Higgins gasped in pain. "It's his appendix," the doctor said. "He'll have to have an emergency operation."

So on April 1, 1945, Ed Higgins lay in sickbay, recovering from his operation. But on that same day his frogmen comrades guided the first landing craft ashore on Okinawa, just as they had guided the first ones to other islands. Then, back on their APDs, many of them manned machine guns during the long weeks of the fiercest air-sea battle in all history.

During those weeks the Japanese sent more than a thousand suicide planes to strike at the American fleet. Before the battle was over these planes had sunk 24 ships, damaged 202 others, and killed more than 1,000 American sailors. But Okinawa was captured.

On August 6, 1945, American B-29s, flying from bases the frogmen had helped to conquer, dropped the first atom bomb on Hiroshima. Three days later they dropped another on Nagasaki. Less than a month later, on September 2, General MacArthur accepted Japan's formal surrender.

The Korean War—
SCUBA Joins UDT

When the Second World War ended, the United States Navy had thirty-three Underwater Demolition Teams in combat or in training. But as happens at the end of every war, most of the men wanted to go home as soon as the fighting was over. Americans hoped there would never be another war, and had no desire to maintain a large army or navy. So by 1948 the Navy had only four UDTs, and these were at only half their combat strength. Two were stationed on the East Coast, two on the West.

With no immediate war to fight, these men began to study the lessons of World War II and to try to devise new and better methods for the future. Lieutenant Commander Douglas Fane, who had taken part in the Okinawa invasion, was sent to Europe to study the underwater work of the British, Italians and Germans. After he returned to this country, he was placed in command of the two UDTs on the East Coast. Here he began to experiment with various types of SCUBA, the abbreviation for "self-

UDT men conduct a reconnaissance along the rocky Korean coast.

contained underwater breathing apparatus." Other frogmen went on a naval exploration of the Antarctic. Still others began to experiment with working from submarines.

Then, suddenly, the United States found itself involved in another war—this time in the small Asian peninsula of Korea, approximately 125 miles from the islands of Japan.

During World War II, Korea had been under the control of Japan. When the war ended, the northern part of the peninsula was occupied by Russian troops; the southern half, by United States soldiers. By the time the occupation troops were withdrawn, the country had been divided artificially into two sections. North Korea, a neighbor of Red China and the U.S.S.R., was under communist domination, while South Korea had set up a new and somewhat uncertain democracy.

In June of 1950, highly trained North Korean troops invaded the southern half of the peninsula without warning. Quickly the United Nations, with the United States supplying a large proportion of the men and money, went to the aid of South Korea. And so, just five years after the end of World War II, America was at war again.

General Douglas MacArthur was placed in command of the United Nations forces. But before his army could reach Korea in any numbers, the North Koreans had overrun a large part of South Korea. The only seaport available to MacArthur was Pusan. Soon it was hopelessly overcrowded, both with troops on the way to battle, and with Korean refugees fleeing from the advancing Communists. MacArthur decided to use a beach seventy miles north of Pusan —if the beach proved suitable.

Scouting it was a job for an Underwater Demolition Team. There was no team available, but a UDT lieutenant named George Atcheson was in Japan. He was flown to the little town of Pohang in Korea, and taken out to the beach in a jeep. Here, along with some army swimmers, he went up and down the beach, out to deep water and back again. As minutely as possible he and his companions mapped the shore and its approaches.

A few days later the Navy put 10,000 U.N. soldiers and their supplies ashore here. And just two days after landing, these soldiers met the advancing North Koreans and stopped them.

Up until this point the war had gone steadily in favor of the North Koreans. Now the battle turned. United Nations troops, most of them American or South Korean, began to drive northward up the long, narrow peninsula.

In this advance General MacArthur used the same

141

end-run technique he had used in the South Pacific
—sending troops to make amphibious landings behind the enemy lines. And once again this meant
work for the UDTs, who were set to exploring
beaches as they had done against the Japanese.

There was also a new and even more dangerous
job. Many of the roads and railroads that supplied
the North Koreans ran close along the shore. The
country was very rough, and the roads went across
many bridges and through tunnels. So a quickly
gathered Underwater Demolition unit joined with a
Marine unit under Major Edward Dupras to make
commando raids behind the enemy lines.

An APD, the *Horace A. Bass,* carried the men far
up the coastline to where aerial photographs had
shown a railroad tunnel within a few hundred yards
of the beach. At night the APD moved to within
two miles of shore. Rubber boats were loaded with
more than a ton of explosives; then marines and
frogmen paddled silently toward the land. A few
hundred yards from the beach some of the frogmen
went into the water and began to swim ahead. They
reached the water's edge and lay there a few
minutes, listening and looking. There was no sign
of the enemy, so with their flashlights shielded in
such a way that they could not be seen from the
land, the frogmen signaled the boats to come ahead.

Once the boats were on the beach, the marines started to advance. But at this point a North Korean guard suddenly appeared out of the darkness. For an instant he and one of the UDT men faced one another, only a few feet apart. The frogman still wore his diving mask; he was semi-naked, painted black-and-green for camouflage. The Korean took one wild look, dropped his gun, and fled.

"We ought to have him on our side," the UDT man said later. "He got away from there even faster than a fuse puller could have done."

But the fleeing Korean was bound to sound the alarm, so the job had to be finished in a hurry. Swiftly the marines spread out to form a picket line while the frogmen, staggering under their loads of TNT, hurried to the railroad. They loaded a hundred feet of track with explosives, then piled explosives inside the mouth of the tunnel.

When everything was ready, the signal was given. Marines and frogmen retreated to the beach, except for Major Dupras and UDT lieutenants P. A. Wilson and George Atcheson. These men were the fuse pullers. They cut the fuse to allow themselves a few minutes, then ran almost as fast as the North Korean guard had done.

The rubber boats were already in the water. The officers piled in, and the men began to paddle furiously. They were two hundred yards off the beach when the railroad and the tunnel exploded.

While this team of commando frogmen continued to raid up and down the coast, other UDTs found themselves in a new version of an old job. The city of Wonsan had been recaptured by South Korean troops, but a number of small surrounding islands were still in Communist hands. The narrow channel to the harbor ran between these islands, and the North Koreans had sown thousands of mines in both the channel and the bay. There were so many that the United Nations forces did not have enough mine sweepers to clear them. So frogmen and a Navy helicopter were sent to help. The helicopter would spot the mines, which had been moored just a few feet below the surface. Then the UDT men would come as close as they dared in a small boat, dive over and either put a buoy on the mine or cut it free and explode it with rifle fire. In their first afternoon's work they destroyed dozens of mines.

Things did not go so well the next day. Two of the mine sweepers, within a few moments of one another, struck mines and exploded. As they caught fire and began to sink, the nearby UDT men rushed to help rescue the wounded.

At this point North Korean artillery concealed on

Wearing rubber suits to protect them from frigid Korean waters, UDT men paddle their way through heavily mined Wonsan harbor.

two nearby islands began to fire. While shells burst around the sinking ships, the UDT men carried off the wounded. They put so many on one boat that there was no room for the frogmen. They had to swim.

Because the mine sweepers had gone down so swiftly, there had been no chance to save their secret code books. To make sure these could never fall into Communist hands, the frogmen went back again the next day. The ships had sunk in about 100 feet of water, so William Giannotti, wearing an aqualung, went down to look for them.

Giannotti found the sunken ships all right, but there was no way to reach the code books. In order to make sure they were destroyed, other frogmen went down with explosives. The mine sweepers were demolished. Then the ocean bottom was raked until all the fragments had sunk into the muck forever.

By this time a two-piece rubber suit was a common part of the UDT uniform—and not a bit too soon. As winter came on, the weather got colder and colder. The men clearing the thousands of mines from Wonsan sometimes had ice form on their suits when they climbed out of the water. The suits were not perfect. Frequently they leaked. But they made possible work that could not have been done otherwise.

Toward the end of 1950 the whole aspect of the Korean War changed again. MacArthur's United Nations army had pushed the North Korean forces back almost to the North Korean-Chinese border. As a fighting unit, the North Korean army was destroyed.

Then, unexpectedly, the Chinese began to pour their troops into Korea. There was, however, no declaration of war by Red China. The Chinese soldiers were supposed to be "volunteers" helping the North Koreans of their own free will, and not representatives of the Chinese government. So General MacArthur was under orders not to attack beyond the Chinese border. He could not even bomb the supply lines rushing reinforcements into North Korea. Since it was impossible to fight a war where the enemy had only to duck across a line to be safe, the U.N. forces fell back and set up their defenses across the middle of the country.

The Korean conflict dragged on for dreary months, still bloody but getting nowhere. Now one of the main jobs of the UDTs was to land South Korean guerrilla fighters by boat behind the Communist lines, and later rescue them again. Another job was destroying fish nets.

Fish made up a large part of the Koreans' food. And the Chinese armies, having little surplus food, also relied heavily on the North Korean fish supply. Most of these fish were caught in nets; some were so large they had to be hauled up by machines.

So American ships ranged up and down the Korean coast looking for fish nets. When they found them, the frogmen would slip in at night in their

(Above) During Operation Fish-net a frogman leaps into the water while another UDT man adjusts his goggles as he waits his turn. (Left) UDT men hang out captured North Korean fish nets to dry.

small boats, dive over and destroy the nets.

It was a strange war. But eventually the Communist attempt to take over all of Korea was thwarted, and on July 27, 1953, an Armistice Agreement was signed.

UDT Today

At the time the very first UDTs were being trained, Lieutenant Commander Kauffman, who was later to become an admiral, told his men, "I promise you that I will do everything in my power to make sure this school graduates no officer I would not be glad to follow myself as an enlisted man. And I hope we will turn out no enlisted man I would not want in a unit under my command."

That same statement is being used today in the two schools where the United States Navy trains its frogmen of tomorrow. These schools are located at Little Creek, Virginia, and at Coronado, California. They are probably the roughest, toughest schools in all the armed services. Every man must be a volunteer from some other branch of the Navy. They know ahead of time that the course is going to be rough. Yet only about thirty percent of those who volunteer manage to last it out and win their "swim fins," just as pilots earn their wings.

The first two weeks are devoted almost entirely

A Navy frogman hits the water with the Mark V mixed-gas SCUBA.

to physical exercise. The men are divided into squads, and each squad lives with a rubber boat that it carries wherever it goes—in and out of the ocean, along the beach, even to the mess hall. They learn to ride it through the surf to the beach, to push and pull and fight it back through the surf to open water again. There are hours and hours of calisthenics.

Chief Boatswain's Mate John Parrish, who saw combat with the frogmen at Guam and again in the Philippines, later became an instructor in the school at Little Creek. "The purpose of the first two weeks of training," Chief Parrish has said, "is to get the men tough enough so they can survive the next three weeks. That's when the going really gets rough."

In these next weeks the hours of calisthenics get longer and longer, and harder and harder. The men are routed out of bed at all hours to go on double-time marches. They run through the deep sand of beaches, crawl through swamps, plunge in and out of the ocean. They may get back to their quarters, anticipating a good night's sleep, only to be routed out again after two or three hours to run an obstacle course that contains everything from barbed wire fences to two slack wires stretched high above a muddy creek. The men try to cross over the creek on one wire while holding onto the other, which is five or six feet above it. The upper wire is con-

Frogman trainees attempt to cross over a creek without falling into the mud and water below.

During an amphibious assault landing exercise, UDT men set up explosives on "enemy-constructed" obstacles.

stantly being tightened and loosened, so that eventually the man is almost sure to be dumped off into the mud and water twenty feet below.

About this time the men start to learn some of the secrets of their business, which includes not only swimming but also the use of explosives. Some men have an instinctive fear of high explosives, just as others have a fear of snakes or spiders. Such a man must learn to overcome that fear or else get out of the UDTs.

The fifth week of training is known as Hell Week. "And that," according to Chief Parrish, "is just what

it is." Into this one final week is packed all the training of the previous four weeks. The men are deliberately worked to the point of utter exhaustion. They are allowed little sleep.

On the last day, comes the climax, which is a simulated attack on an enemy-held beach. The men approach in rubber boats while previously planted explosives blow up all around them. They fight through the surf to the beach with more explosives going off everywhere. Sand and debris rain down on them. The deafening explosions keep going on and on, like an enemy bombardment. In the midst of

155

this simulated bombardment, the men must cross the beach and plant their own explosives, destroying the barriers which have been set up for them.

Yet even then it is not over. When they are at the point of physical collapse the men are assigned one more job. "It's a job that is impossible to accomplish," according to Chief Parrish. "Or at least almost impossible. Because we want to know how a man will react when, already exhausted, he is faced with what looks like certain defeat. We want to know if he will keep trying or not."

The Underwater Demolition schools at Little Creek and Coronado receive a great many letters from persons who have heard about their program. Many are from boys who are interested in becoming Navy frogmen. And many come from persons who claim the schools are cruel and inhuman and ought to be abolished.

The United States Navy, however, believes this kind of training is necessary. The frogmen work as teams, but they are comparatively small teams. In wartime, if one man should falter and turn back without accomplishing his mission, he might endanger the lives of hundreds; he might even turn the tide of battle.

There is an old nursery rhyme that goes: "For

want of a nail the shoe was lost. For want of a shoe the horse was lost. For want of a horse the rider was lost. For want of a rider the battle was lost. For want of a battle the nation was lost. And all for the want of a horseshoe nail."

The Navy does not want one of its frogmen to be that horseshoe nail.

Most of the men who drop out of the Underwater Demolition schools (and remember that only about thirty percent manage to stick it out) do so during these first five weeks. "They lose desire," Chief Parrish has said. "You can see the light die out of their eyes."

Yet a man does not have to be particularly big or powerful to get through the course. In fact most of the frogmen are not unusually large. What a future demolitioneer must have is endurance and determination and courage. He must be able to take a beating, yet keep on going, to face defeat and still try and try again.

Nor does the future frogman need to be an unusually good swimmer. At least not at first. The Navy will teach him that. Some men have gone through UDT training who could scarcely swim at all when they first arrived at the school.

After those first five weeks at the Underwater Demolition schools, the training becomes less strenuous physically, but more technical.

John Synge, the Irish poet and playwright, once wrote in a book about the Aran Islands: "A man who is not afraid of the sea will soon be drowned, for he will be going out on a day he should not. But we do be afraid of the sea, and we do only be drowned now and then."

The Underwater Demolition schools teach their men to be afraid of the sea in the proper way. They learn to swim for miles on the surface, and they learn to swim under water using all types of equipment. They also learn the difference between one kind of SCUBA and another, and when and where each should be used. They learn the effect of underwater pressure on the human body and the effect of the different gases in the different aqualungs. They learn what a man can do safely, and what he can't do safely. When one frogman was asked to name the most dangerous thing about his job, he replied immediately, "Breaking the rules, or not knowing them. If you know the rules and don't break them, you are safe."

Since the end of the war, tremendous advances have been made in UDT techniques. Underwater craft, somewhat like the pigs that the Italians rode into Alexandria harbor, have been vastly improved. Carrying one or two men, they can scoot about under water almost like planes in the air. Such craft will allow a demolitioneer not only to tow more explosives than he could swimming, but also to pull them much faster and over longer distances.

Frogmen have learned how to leave a submerged submarine, and also how to reënter while it is still submerged. If necessary a frogman can now approach an enemy beach in a submarine, leave it wearing SCUBA and swim in to the beach. He can explore along the waterline and then return to the submarine without either the craft or the man ever appearing on the surface.

During World War II it became obvious that the frogman was most exposed to danger while in the small boats that brought him within swimming distance of the beach and then took him away again. So ever since the war's end, the Navy has been experimenting with new methods of launching and recovering swimmers. One of these has been by parachute. Most of the men who finish Underwater Demolition school now go on to a parachute jumping school, where they become experts at low-altitude jumping.

But modern frogmen can do more than leap *into* the water from a plane. They can also be recovered *from* the water by a plane. For this the frogman inflates a balloon with helium from a small bottle. The

As part of a training reconnaissance mission, a Navy frogman jumps from a hovering helicopter into waters near an enemy beach.

balloon is attached to five hundred feet of light, braided nylon line; the other end of the line is fastened to the frogman's parachute harness.

With the inflated balloon floating five hundred feet over his head, the frogman takes a kind of sitting position in the water. His back is turned to the approaching airplane. The plane has a special hook that catches the nylon line just below the balloon. By this method the man is lifted straight out of the water. Indeed, men have been picked up from land as well as from water in this way. Once in the air, the line is reeled into the plane by a large winch.

The most spectacular peacetime work of the frogmen, however, has been in two new fields: in space, and in the frozen reaches of the Arctic and Antarctic oceans.

It is the frogman's new mobility, his ability to work in both sea and air, that has made him of such value to the space program. Now the United States Air Force sends parachute jumpers to the frogmen schools just as the frogmen go to parachute schools. More than once frogmen have saved a capsule from a satellite after it has plunged into the ocean. To do this the capsule must be quickly located by a circling plane. Frogmen bail out. In the water they dive and fasten buoys to the capsule before it can sink. Then they inflate life rafts of their own and sit guard until a ship can arrive to take both the capsule and them aboard. Once Air Force frogmen spent eighteen hours floating alongside a satellite nose cone. Without them the cone and its precious scientific cargo would have been lost.

This happened in the warm Pacific waters near Hawaii. Half a world away other frogmen were swimming under icebergs in the Arctic Ocean.

Commander Francis Douglas Fane, who with Don Moore has written a thrilling book about Navy frogmen, called *The Naked Warriors*, was the first to suggest that a man might be able to swim in arctic waters. Some people thought he was crazy. But he clung to his idea and kept experimenting to find a suit that would make such work possible.

When the United States began to establish its DEW (Distant Early Warning) line of radar stations across the top of the world the need for arctic frogmen became obvious.

The radar operators could be flown in to their stations, but ships were needed to bring in supplies. There were no harbors, however, and the arctic waters were crowded with icebergs. In addition, nobody knew about the beaches and whether or not small craft could be brought into them.

So frogmen went north.

In their first experiments, the frogmen wore rubber suits with heavy underwear beneath. They dived with lines attached to them, so they could be hauled back to the ship in case they became too cold to swim. But soon they learned that men could swim, for a short time anyway, even in twenty-seven-degree water—water so cold it would have frozen solid if it had not been salty.

Yet there was always the danger of a rubber suit's tearing. Once it began to leak, once the icy water got inside, a swimmer could not live for long. So a new suit—called a "wet" suit—was developed. Made of a substance like foam rubber, this suit contained innumerable tiny air pockets. Worn inside the solid rubber, or "dry" suit, the wet suit gave added warmth as well as protection against leaks. Even if water seeped through the outer suit, the little air pockets of the wet suit still retained some of the body warmth. With it frogmen could work in the coldest water for a full hour.

There is a great deal of work for frogmen to do on these arctic expeditions. Ships crowding in through the ice fields often damage their hulls or

To test the performance of his underwater equipment, an arctic frogman descends through a hole cut in the ice.

propellers. Since there are no dry docks where the ships can be taken for overhaul, frogmen dive among the icebergs to make emergency repairs.

Arctic frogmen also explore the rocky beaches near the radar stations, not once but year after year. This is necessary because each winter huge ice floes grind against the shore, sometimes pushing in new rocks and sometimes carrying away old ones. The beach is therefore constantly changing.

Frogmen have accompanied the atomic submarines on their history-making voyages across the North Pole. They have swum under icebergs so the Navy could better understand how they were formed. Lieutenant Commander Robert Terry, a young veteran of arctic expeditions, once swam a quarter of a mile beneath solid ice. He reported that, seen from beneath, it was a beautiful diamond-blue color.

Before the frogmen arrived in the far north, most Eskimos had never seen a man swim. This led to a strange adventure for two demolitioneers.

One day Lieutenant Charles Aquadro, a frogman as well as a naval doctor, was swimming with a friend near their arctic camp. They were off duty, swimming just for the fun of it and testing some new suits, when they decided to visit a nearby Eskimo village. There were a number of small ice floes on the way. Aquadro and his friend would climb onto one of these, crawl across it on hands and knees, and slip into the water on the far side. Then they would swim to the next ice floe and climb over it.

As they approached the Eskimo village, someone saw them. Dogs began to howl and there was a great deal of shouting and running around. Then, suddenly, they heard the sound of a gun. A bullet struck the ice between the two men and went zooming off. Then another bullet.

For a moment Dr. Aquadro could not understand why the friendly Eskimos should be trying to kill them. Then he realized—the Eskimos thought they were seals, and good eating! Immediately the frogmen stripped off their masks. They began to jump up and down and do some very loud shouting. "Seals can be pretty noisy themselves," Dr. Aquadro said later. "But none of them ever made as much noise as we did."

It was an adventure typical for men of the United States Navy's Underwater Demolition Teams. For these are men whose work is hard and dangerous, but also exciting and interesting. They are also men who prove in their work that no matter how complex modern war, or modern living, may become there are always times when the final outcome will depend, not on machinery, but on the skill and courage and spirit of the individual human being.

Index

About the Author

WYATT BLASSINGAME first became interested in the U.S. Navy's Underwater Demolition Teams during World War II while he was serving as an intelligence officer with the Naval Air Corps on the islands of Tinian and Okinawa. After the war he was called back for two weeks' duty in Washington, and there he heard Commander Draper Kauffman talk about the work of the UDT. These experiences led to his interest in writing a book about the impressive activities of the U.S. frogmen.

For many years now Mr. Blassingame has lived on the island of Anna Maria, off the west coast of Florida. In addition to having contributed stories and articles to such magazines as *Harper's* and the *Saturday Evening Post,* he has written four adult novels, as well as numerous books for young readers. Among the latter is a World Landmark, *The French Foreign Legion;* other popular nonfiction titles for young readers are *The First Book of Florida, His Kingdom for a Horse,* and *They Rode the Frontier.*

U. S. LANDMARK BOOKS

World Landmark Books